The Fate of American Poetry

The Fate of American

POETRY

Jonathan
Holden

The University of Georgia Press

Athens and London

© 1991 by the University of Georgia Press
Athens, Georgia 30602
All rights reserved
Designed by Louise M. Jones
Set in 10/13 Sabon by Tseng Information Systems, Inc.
Printed and bound by Thomson-Shore, Inc.
The paper in this book meets the guidelines for
permanence and durability of the Committee on
Production Guidelines for Book Longevity of the
Council on Library Resources.

Printed in the United States of America

95 94 93 92 91   C   5 4 3 2 1
95 94 93 92 91   P   5 4 3 2 1

Library of Congress Cataloging in Publication Data
Holden, Jonathan.
The fate of American poetry / Jonathan Holden.
p.   cm.
Includes bibliographical references and index.
ISBN 0-8203-1364-5 (alk. paper)
ISBN 0-8203-1398-X (pbk.: alk. paper)
1. American poetry—20th century—History and criticism.
I. Title.
PS325.H57   1991
811'.5409—dc20   91-12069
                                                CIP

British Library Cataloging in Publication Data available

Contents

Acknowledgments

"Seals in the Inner Harbor": From *Seals in the Inner Harbor* by Brendan Galvin. First published by Carnegie Mellon University Press in 1986. Reprinted by permission of the publisher.

"Bess," "Ceremony," and "Thinking for Berky": From *Stories That Could Be True* by William Stafford. Copyright 1977 by William Stafford. Published by Harper & Row. Reprinted by permission of the author.

"Harbor Seals": From *The Theology of Doubt* by Scott Cairns. Copyright 1985 by Scott Cairns. Published by Cleveland State University Press. Reprinted by permission of the author.

"Middle Class Poem": From *Not Dancing* by Stephen Dunn. First published by Carnegie Mellon University Press in 1984. Reprinted by permission of the publisher.

"The Fall of the Human Empire": From *Good Trembling* by Baron Wormser. Copyright 1985 by Baron Wormser. Reprinted by permission of Houghton Mifflin Co. and Thomas S. Hart, Literary Enterprises.

"The Gas Station": From *Poems: 1963–1983* by C. K. Williams. Copyright 1989 by C. K. Williams. First published by Farrar, Straus & Giroux. Reprinted by permission of Farrar, Straus & Giroux and Bloodaxe Books.

"Acquainted with the Night": From *The Poetry of Robert Frost* edited by Edward Connery Lathem. Copyright 1928, 1969 by Holt, Rinehart and Winston. Copyright 1956 by Robert Frost. Reprinted by permission of Henry Holt and Company, Inc.; Jonathan Cape Ltd.; and the Estate of Robert Frost.

"Palo Alto: The Marshes": From *Field Guide* by Robert Hass. Copyright 1973 by Robert Haas. Published by Yale University Press. Reprinted by permission.

"Buying and Selling": From *A Walk with Tom Jefferson* by Philip Levine. Copyright 1988 by Philip Levine. Reprinted by permission of Alfred A. Knopf, Inc.

Introduction

In the August 1988 issue of *Commentary*, in his essay "Who Killed Poetry?" Joseph Epstein attempted to describe the situation of American poetry in 1988. After sketching accurately how poetry is "published" in America—by poetry readings that take place mainly at universities and in books mainly by university presses ("Sometimes it seems as if there isn't a poem written in this nation that isn't subsidized or underwritten by a grant either from a foundation or the government or a teaching salary or a fellowship of one kind or another"), he says:

> Contemporary poetry is no longer a part of the regular intellectual diet. People of general intellectual interests who feel that they ought to read or at least to know about works on modern society or recent history or novels that attempt to convey something about the way we live now, no longer feel the same compunction about contemporary poetry. . . . poetry no longer seems in any way where the action is. It begins to seem, in fact, a sideline activity.[1]

The alleged "sideline" position of poetry in American culture, according to Epstein, is the result of the modernist movement and of "professionalism." Of the modernists, he writes: "New, too, was their attitude toward the reader, whom they, perhaps first among any writers in history, chose in a radical way to disregard. . . . If what they wrote was uncompromisingly difficult, they did not see this as their problem."[2]

Modernism leads to Epstein's main indictment, professional-ism:

> whereas one tended to think of the modernist poet as an artist—even
> if he worked hard in a bank in London, or at an insurance company
> in Hartford, or in a Physician's office in Rutherford, New Jersey—
> one tends to think of the contemporary poet as a professional: a
> poetry professional. Like a true professional, he is rather insulated
> within the world of his fellow-professionals. The great majority of
> poets today live in an atmosphere almost entirely academic, but it is
> academic with a difference: not the world of science and scholarship
> but that of the creative-writing program and the writing workshop.[3]

The comfy professional status of poets in universities combined
with "the encouraging, the somewhat therapeutic atmosphere of
the workshop" have, in Epstein's view, contributed to "lowering
the high standard of work which is poetry's only serious claim
on anyone's attention," resulting in "a great deal of contemporary poetry" that is "slightly political, heavily preening, and not
distinguished enough in language or subtlety of thought to be
memorable."
Epstein asks, rhetorically:

> Is it all up with poetry, then? As early as the 1940's, Edmund Wilson
> wrote an essay carrying the questioning title, "Is Verse a Dying Tech-
> nique?" Wilson's answer was, essentially, yes, it is. Prose, in Wilson's
> view, had overwhelmed poetry . . . Wilson does allow that our lyric
> poets may be compared with any who have ever written. . . ."[4]

Epstein concedes that:

> Poets have not altogether given up on telling stories . . . for the most
> part contemporary poetry has gone off in the direction of the lyric. In
> practice this means a shortish poem, usually fewer than forty lines,
> generally describing an incident or event or phenomenon of nature or
> work of art or relationship or emotion, in more or less distinguished
> language, the description often, though not always, yielding a slightly
> oblique insight.[5]

His concession, however, is a reluctant one:

> But in taking up the lyric as its chief form, contemporary poetry has
> seriously delimited itself. It thereby gives away much that has always
> made literature an activity of primary significance; it gives away the
> power to tell stories, to report on how people live and have lived, to
> struggle for those larger truths about life the discovery of which is
> the final justification for reading. . . .[6]

In his brilliant study of the history of free verse, *Missing Measures* (1990), Timothy Steele repeats Epstein's complaint, placing it in a more fully elaborated context:

> The last two hundred years . . . mark a change. Many of the finest fic-
> tion writers of the age compose in prose rather than in meter, and the
> modern novel acquires a popularity and respectability formerly ac-
> corded to epic, verse drama, and lyric. . . . Modern poets commonly
> urge that poetry has lost much of its material, it must assimilate
> characteristics of the novel. Whereas in earlier times prose writers ex-
> perimented with incorporating verse cadences into prose, poets now
> begin to experiment with integrating the relative rhythms of prose
> into verse. Prose becomes, in short, the primary art.[7]

Epstein and Steele are correct in saying that the "lyric" is the "chief form" of contemporary poetry; but Epstein's description of a "lyric" is an invidious one both in what it leaves out and in that it is supported by no examples. In fact, it is virtually meaningless. It is "a shortish poem." The remainder of his definition could apply not only to *any* poem but to any reasonably good work of fiction. Consider, for example, Brendan Galvin's "Seals in the Inner Harbor." This poem is, as Epstein would have it, "a shortish poem . . . fewer than forty lines, . . . describing an incident or event or phenomenon of nature . . . in more or less distinguished language . . . yielding a slightly oblique insight":

> Ducks, at first, except they didn't
> fly when we rounded the jetty
> and swung into the channel.

didn't spread panic among themselves,
peeling the whole flock off the water,
but followed, popping under
and poking up as if to study our faces
for someone, their eyes rounded still
by the first spearing shock of ice,
or amazed to find our white town
here again, backed by a steeple
telling the hours in sea time.
Their skeptical brows seemed from a day
when men said a green Christmas
would fill this harbor with dead
by February. We left them hanging
astern at world's edge, afloat on
summer's afterlife: gray jetty,
water and sky, the one gray vertical
of smoke rising straight from a chimney
across the cove. We could believe
they were men who had dragged
this bottom till its shells were smooth
and round as gift shop wampum,
who never tied up and walked away
a final time, but returned for evenings
like this was going to be, thirsting
for something to fight salt off with,
needing a place to spit and plan
the rescue of children's children.[8]

What is one to say? Galvin's language is distinctly above the "more or less distinguished." Passages like "spread panic among themselves, / peeling the whole flock off the water," are like the best descriptions by Thoreau, "scientifically" exact, yet superior to scientific observation alone: they are alive with the rhythm and shape of what they describe. In its revelation of the contingency of human life and sea life—how the "skeptical brows" of the two

domains, so alien to one another, regard each other, mutually acknowledge one another—as if the numbers of fishermen lost at sea
might resurface as seals—"Seals in the Inner Harbor" moves me
greatly, and the phrase "Inner Harbor" creates additional reso-
nances. "Inner Harbor" hints at the human subconscious, which,
many would say, remains our most direct link to the natural world,
the world of pure instinct. The seals' heads "poking up" from the
waters of the subconscious resemble the unbidden but reassertive
phenomena of dream-work. "Seals in the Inner Harbor" does not
"report on how people live and have lived" with the exhaustive
documentary detail of a novel or short story. But it accomplishes
tasks that most prose fiction doesn't.

One of the basic assumptions that one makes when starting out
to write anything involves choice of genre. The implicit axiom behind one's choice is this: that each artistic medium, each literary
genre has evolved in such a way that it, alone, is better adapted to
accomplish certain tasks than any other genre. This is an axiom,
of course, unprovable. But, like the axioms on which, for example,
a geometry is founded, it permits the poet, the fictionist, the jour-
nalist, the essayist, the minister considering a sermon, to get into
action, to invent. When Epstein maintains that "the lyric" is the
"chief form" of "contemporary poetry," and that our poetry has
thus "seriously delimited itself," his definition of "lyric" is sim-
plistic. There *is* no mode of poetry so pure that it could be labeled
simply "lyric." Modes of poetry, like the genres of literature, not
only allude to one another, they partake of one another. For example, Galvin's poem, *does* tell a story, not the kind of story that
a novel, with a wide cast of characters and a variety of settings
might tell, but a story nonetheless. The tasks that a good "lyric" is
adapted to perform are rather more sophisticated and subtle than
merely "describing an incident or event or phenomenon." What
are these tasks? As "Seals in the Inner Harbor" might illustrate,
there appear to be two central ones.

The first—the best-known task and the one implicit in Valery's
famous analogy that poetry is to prose as dance is to walking—

is to exhibit the intrinsic textures of its own medium, language, to "foreground" this medium, bring it into relief. The finest prose writing can do this, of course. Here, for example, is a passage from page 10 of Don DeLillo's novel *White Noise*. The passage is spoken by a character named Murray Jay Suskind, Professor of Popular Culture at the "College-on-the-Hill":

> Heat. This is what cities mean to me. You get off the train and walk out of the station and you are hit with the full blast. The heat of air, traffic and people. The heat of food and sex. The heat of tall build-ings. The heat that floats out of the subways and the tunnels. It's always fifteen degrees hotter in the cities. Heat rises from the side-walks and falls from the poisoned sky. The buses breathe heat. Heat emanates from crowds of shoppers and office workers. The entire infrastructure is based on heat, desperately uses up heat, breeds more heat. The eventual heat death of the universe that scientists love to talk about is already well underway and you can feel it happening all around you in any large or medium-sized city. Heat and wetness.[9]

Beautiful as the DeLillo passage is, a poem like Galvin's has at least one advantage over prose. The vision that "Seals" presents requires no supporting context—it is self-sufficient—and this vision, for all its complexity, has been dramatized with almost incredible economy. The poem's isolation from a supporting con-text, which would be a disadvantage if the poem had been in-tended to communicate a body of factual information about marine biology, or to tell a complex story, is actually an advantage for Galvin, because it brings into high relief both the language of the poem and, more significantly, the *shape* of the experience that the poem describes—a structure which, if buried in the middle of a longer prose passage, would tend to be obscured and go un-noticed. The main task of a good poem like Galvin's is to render, often but not always in miniature, a model of the structure of experience itself. What kinds of experience? Traditionally, the ex-periences are those of initiation, involving love, death, seasonal change, natural process.

The rendering of structure, however, is not the only task that the "shortish poem" can perform. Let us look at a second "lyric." This one, by William Stafford, *does* contain, as Epstein would have it, some of "those larger truths about life the discovery of which is the final justification for reading":

BESS

Ours are the streets where Bess first met her
cancer. She went to work every day past the
secure houses. At her job in the library
she arranged better and better flowers, and when
students asked for books her hand went out
to help. In the last years of her life
she had to keep her friends from knowing
how happy they were. She listened while they
complained about food or work or the weather.
And the great national events danced
their grotesque, fake importance. Always

Pain moved where she moved. She walked
ahead; it came. She hid; it found her.
No one ever served another so truly;
no enemy ever meant so strong a hate.
It was almost as if there was no room
left for her on earth. But she remembered
where joy used to live. She straightened its flowers;
she did not weep when she passed its houses;
and when she finally pulled into a tiny corner
and slipped from pain, her hand opened
again, and the streets opened, and she wished all well.[10]

If Galvin's poem needed little or no critical mediation, this poem needs even less. Its depiction both of the loneliness of pain and of its protagonist's moral courage is nearly overwhelming, and in sentences as memorable and wise as the most potent Biblical scripture: "In the last years of her life / she had to keep her friends from knowing / how happy they were." Although "Bess," like "Seals," is not "lyric" in the sense in which Northrop Frye defines "lyric" as an "overheard utterance," it is "lyric" in Epstein's superficial sense of the word. It is "shortish," and it is spoken by some version of its author. Both poems, however, contain an element of narrative. Lyric "gives away" (to use Epstein's words) less than he admits. Modes of verse are far more flexible and susceptible of combinations than he realizes.

When the speaking persona of a "shortish poem" is different from the author, so that the reader is required to interpolate the circumstances of the speaker and the occasion of his (or her) speech, the verse will acquire a pronounced element of story and avail itself of a wider range of subject-matter—subject matter beyond the personal concerns of the author. "Lyric" will begin to incorporate—to imitate—more of the features of other genres.

To observe this phenomenon, let us look at a third poem. Whereas both the Stafford poem and the Galvin poem are spoken by some version of their author, the "speaker" of this third poem is not. She is a nurse. The poet, Marilyn Krysl, was an artist in residence in the Center for Human Caring, during the 1987–1988 academic year, and this poem appears in her *Midwife and Other Poems on Caring,* published in 1989 by the National League for Nursing:

QUADRIPLEGIC: THE BATH

"You'll feel like
new," I said, keeping things
breezy, as though we all know
how getting clean feels
good, no one in their
right mind
would refuse it, because he looked
like he just might file
a dissenting opinion. Which he could

do. Though he couldn't
get up and go—bye, *sugar buns,*
I'm walking out on you—which is
what he'd have

liked to do. He leaned
back then, the old stinker, like Caesar
in his chariot, and let me see his
penis, that loose fold
of flag that would not
fly again,
and said, "Ma'am, you seem to have
the wrong man. I don't require either your services
or your opinions." I could see

how indeed
neither service nor opinion
would be of the slightest
use to him. "O.K., all
right," I said, hand across
forehead, in mock
shock, letting him know the sharpness of the male
was in him still. "O.K.," I said, "I get
the picture." And I turned away and was
going, leaving him the privacy
he had once, like a general,
commanded. "Aw
shit," he said, and with a wide sweep
drew me in. "You'll catch hell
if you don't do me. Anyway,
I stink. Come on with your
scrub brush."

       So I knelt beside the water
the orderlies had set him in
and began to bathe him.[11]

Politics is about power, and the sexual/political situation dramatized in this poem is far-reaching. The female speaker, who has virtually absolute power over her patient (as a mother has absolute power over her baby), allows him to display, for the sake of his dignity, the charade of a power he no longer has. In forty-three lines, Krysl, with a flourish that is as sympathetic as it is comic, has sketched the traditional arrangement between men and women in America: how power is wielded and negotiated, the cost of this to men, the cost of this to women. She has done more than this. She has sketched vividly two believable characters, and she has told a story, told it in a way that, though abbreviated, has some advantages over prose narration. Her language—"the old stinker, like Caesar / in his chariot," "that loose fold / of flag that would not fly again"—is, partly by virtue of the verse frame alone, but even more significantly because of its prosody and wit, brought into higher relief, rendered more memorable than the language of most prose fiction. In addition, as with the Stafford and Galvin poems, we notice the structure of the experience rendered by Krysl's poem more than we would be likely to notice it if it were embedded in the midst of prose narration.

Working in a given genre, one is inevitably forced to trade some advantages off for others, but the trade-offs are not nearly as severe or as mutually exclusive as critics bemoaning poetry's "marginal" status would have us believe. If Krysl's poem is any indication, verse can handle many of the tasks of prose narration—some characterization, some plot—without sacrificing the structural beauty of "lyric," and it need not be "difficult." "Quadriplegic" could probably interest any serious reader, not just specialists in an English department. To find such poems, however, one must search through a body of published poetry which, with the growth of creative writing pedagogy in America, is of a size unprecedented in human history. As Greg Kuzma stated in "The Catastrophe of Creative Writing," his infamous but grimly accurate review/essay of Martha Collins's *The Catastrophe of Rainbows*: "What is so special about our current scene—so discouraging—is the terrible vastness of the mass, volume, and weight of mediocrity that afflicts us."[12] Joseph Epstein is similarly appalled at the sheer size of the creative-writing industry in America:

> No world I have ever peered in upon can seem simultaneously so smug and so hopeless as that of the world of contemporary poets, especially in its creative-writing program base . . . just now the entire enterprise of poetic creation seems threatened by having been taken out of the world, chilled in the classroom, and vastly overproduced by men and women who are licenced to write it by degree if not necessarily by talent or spirit.[13]

A more sophisticated complaint about both the scale and the institutionalization of poetry writing in contemporary America is that of Charles Altieri, in *Self and Sensibility in Contemporary American Poetry*:

> workshops and the mentality they encourage put poets in a situation closely parallel to that of French painting in the 1850s. There, too, extraordinarily skillful artists created a climate skeptical of any intellectual role for the medium, hence trapping it within a narrow equation of lucidity and elegantly controlled surfaces. Instead of a stress on ideas, there emerged an emphasis on craft that in turn produced a highly inbred professionalism governing both the training of artists and the judgment of their work. Rather than directly seeking sources of patronage among a consuming public, artists received their commissions and praise largely by appealing to other professionals. Their salon juries are our fellowship boards.[14]

Altieri's parallel is arresting, and it is plausible except in one important respect. Although the institutional and "professional" similarities between French painting in the 1850s and American poetry in the 1990s are striking, American poetry in the 1990s is immeasurably more vigorous and varied than nineteenth-century French academic painting.

More puzzling than Altieri's charge of "professionalism" is the criticism which he, a professional academic, evinces at that which is "academic," a criticism of the academy similar to (though milder than) Epstein's disdainful phrasing "chilled in the classroom" (the "classroom" as morgue). Similarly, in his essay "Notes on the New Formalism," Dana Gioia, an excellent poet and also, perhaps, the acutest practical critic in America, wrote:

> All of these revivals of traditional technique (whether or not linked to traditional aesthetics) both reject the specialization and the intellectualization of the arts in the academy over the past forty years and affirm the need for a broader popular audience. The modern movement, which began this century in bohemia, is now ending it in the university, an institution dedicated at least as much to the specialization of knowledge as to its propagation. Ultimately the mission of the university has little to do with the mission of the arts, and this long cohabitation has had an enervating effect on all the arts but especially poetry and music. With the best of intentions the university has intellectualized the arts to a point where they have been cut off from the vulgar vitality of popular traditions and, as a result, their public has shrunk to groups of academic specialists and a captive audience of students, both of whom refer to everything beyond the university as "the real world." Mainly poets read contemporary poetry, and only professional musicians and composers attend concerts of new music.[15]

Nearly everybody in America, regardless of their education (Gioia has an M.A. in Comparative Literature) likes to sneer at school. I do too, even though I make my living in a university. Why, in America, is "school" at any level, such a sitting target for contempt? There are several reasons. The first is a cliché. America is anti-intellectual, "a half savage country" as Pound put it in *Mauberley*. The historical reasons behind such anti-intellectuality I won't presume to guess, except to suggest that the anti-intellectual status quo of American public education (through the twelfth grade) has been institutionalized and maintained by schools of education, staffed by teachers whose course work was primarily in teaching "methods" classes rather than classes of intellectual substance. Most schools of education fear intellectual quality and have contrived what is in effect a massive self-perpetuating lobby, like the N.R.A., to discourage America's best minds—Ph.D.s in the arts and sciences, for example—from entering the teaching ranks. Like many unions, they prefer to run a closed shop.

But why single out *poetry* from all the arts to attack because it is taught in "the classroom"? Epstein and Gioia neglect to mention that in America, colleges and universities are not only the primary patrons of culture and literature, but in fact the last bastions of serious literacy itself. In the state of Kansas, where I live, the university is an oasis in the desert. It is the place where people come, from hundreds of miles around, as in Ray Bradbury's *Fahrenheit 451,* who read *books,* whether the reading be in Differential Topology, in History, in Physics, or, God save us, poetry. Books, not MTV—books that can be carried around and opened on buses, on subways, in bed, on planes, on park benches—are the primary medium for poetry. Isn't it self-evident that the benefits of having universities to provide a reasonably stable patronage, not just for poets but for that dwindling percentage of our population devoted to reading, greatly outweigh the disadvantages? Epstein's and Gioia's complaint about poetry-in-universities reflects the fact that nearly every intellectual I know of (most of them conspicuously less brilliant than Gioia or Epstein) bitches about "the university," bitches about funding, bitches about the eternal decline in standards—bitches in an almost obligatory way, as children, secure in the comforts of home, bitch about their parents. One of the privileges of life—and certainly of free speech—is the privilege to bite the hand that feeds one—to bite that hand especially if it is safe to do so, to bite it *because* it is safe to do so. Indeed, it is a time-honored (though trite) method of self-promotion to set oneself above the university, to criticize the pedantry and complacency of the Establishment. All of the professions, of course, are ridden with pedantry and complacency, but the academic establishment, because it is devoted to the ideals of self-examination and critical thinking, is the safest one to criticize.

As in Gioia's and Epstein's criticism of the academic world, there is inevitable truth to Kuzma's, Epstein's, and Altieri's concern about mediocrity; but to offer a blanket condemnation, as Epstein does, of the "creative-writing program base" of American poetry as "hopeless" is to succumb to what is probably the most insidious temptation for a critic—the temptation to scan the forest, make grand generalizations about it, while losing sight of the trees. When an art form is produced en masse, most of it will conform to the fashion of the moment, be merely competent. But why feign surprise or disappointment at this? Mediocrity is present in every human endeavor. Indeed, it is prevalent *by definition*, it is a statistical fact: In every statistical sample, there is a "median," "the value, equaled or exceeded by exactly half of the values in a given list." To decry "mediocrity" in any list—a list of restaurants, baseball players, attorneys, poets—is redundant.

This book attempts to answer the concerns of the doomsayers on their own ground. It is seeking to identify the exceptional, extract it from the mass, bring it to public attention and thereby to confront directly Epstein's main charge that "contemporary poetry has seriously delimited itself." It will seek to demonstrate, in concrete detail, the opposite: how, in postwar America, our poetry, shedding the elitist vestiges of modernism, has, along with the democratization of higher education in general, enlarged both its capabilities and its audience. The basis of the "broader popular audience" which Gioia dreams of—which all poets dream of—*is* the university. Although our poetry will never acquire, in America, the mass audience that some popular novelists, TV evangelists, journalists, essayists, and popular singers enjoy, it can accommodate with surprising fluency the types of subject matter we find in novels, sermons, and essays. In fact, verse, through its structural conventions and prosodic capabilities, can present this subject matter differently than the other competing genres can, but with its own kind of charm. That is the possibility which this book will examine, after mapping, in its introductory chapters the contemporary milieu. Is the power of poetry really as diminished as Epstein claims? I will look at the evidence: not the forest, but the trees.

Poetry,
more than ever,
is harnessed by
and subordinate to
its criticism.
—The Reaper

1

The State of the Art

In his essay "The Specialization of Poetry" published in the *Hudson Review* in 1975, Wendell Berry voiced many of the same concerns of Altieri, Epstein, and Gioia. Indeed, Berry's term *specialist* was, in context, virtually synonymous with Epstein's term *professional*. Berry wrote:

> Because of the proliferation of so-called protest poetry, and the widespread involvement of poets in public issues, after about 1964, it became possible to suppose that . . . the effort of many poets to speak out against public outrage might recover some of the lost estate of poetry. . . . But the political "involvement" of poets appears, now, to have subsided, leaving the "effective range and influence" of poetry no larger than before. . . . Poetry remains a specialized art, its range and influence so constricted that poets have very nearly become their own audience.
>
> The primary aspect of specialization is practical; the specialist withdraws from responsibility for everything not comprehended by his specialty. . . . What we have too frequently now—in the words of hundreds of poetry reviews in the time of my coming of age—is the notion that what distinguishes a writer from a non-writer is, first and last, a gift and a love of *language*. He is not, that is, distinguished by his knowledge or character or vision or inspiration or the story he has to tell; he is distinguished by his specialty.[1]

Berry then, using quotations from interviews with poets as evidence, accused the specialist poet of disregard for "the issues of traditional form," and suggested that the contemporary poet-specialist has cultivated a poetry of sensibility. He issued the following warning:

> The danger may not be so much in the overcultivation of sensibility as in its *exclusive* cultivation. Sensibility becomes the inescapable stock in trade of the isolated poet who is increasingly cut off from both song and story because the nature of these is communal. . . .
>
> I find it impossible to believe that song can come from or lead to a sense of isolation. . . . But even more suggestive of the specialization of contemporary poets is their estrangement from story telling.[2]

Berry's conclusion summed up his assessment of the situation of poetry in the following cautionary terms:

> There is in reality no such choice as Yeats's "perfection of the life, or of the work." The decision to sacrifice either one of them for the sake of the other becomes ultimately the fatal disease of both. . . .
> The *use* of life to perfect work is an evil of the specialized intellect. It makes of the most humane of disciplines an exploitive industry.[3]

Although Berry's polemic in the preceding passage is an extreme one—issuing from the same mind that would abolish not only the automobile but technology in general—his description of American poetry as an "industry" contains more than a grain of truth. Indeed, it is essential to acknowledge the "industrial" nature of American poetry since the mid-sixties, and also the reasons behind it, if one is to fully appreciate the main trends in American poetry in the 1990s; for the issues underlying this poetry are the immediate result—or reaction to—the situation of poetry during the late sixties and early seventies.

The situation of American poetry in 1960 has been aptly summarized by the poet/critic David Wojahn in his essay " 'Yes, But . . .' Some Thoughts on the New Formalism":

Imagine that it's 1960. You're a twenty-year-old college student, and you fancy yourself a poet . . . the large state university where you study has no course offerings in what later will be called "Creative Writing." Your knowledge of poetry comes exclusively from your reading. You've read a little bit in the tradition of English poetry—some Donne, perhaps, and some Marvell, and you know a little bit about the work of the high moderns: Stevens, Williams, Pound, and surely Eliot. . . . browsing in your local bookstore, you purchase two recent anthologies of younger poets. What confusion you encounter as you read them.

You first page through a little volume edited by three highly re-garded younger writers, Donald Hall, Robert Pack, and Louis Simpson. The book, entitled *New Poets of England and America* . . . includes work by some fifty poets born between 1917 and 1935. After your acquaintance with Williams and Pound, you find the poets represented in the collection to be a humdrum group. The models for the poems are as often as not the Metaphysical poets. . . .

Setting aside *New Poets of England and America*, you begin to look through Donald Allen's *The New American Poetry*. . . . And the poems in the collection certainly *look* different from the ones in *New Poets of England and America*. Only one poet in the volume, Robert Creeley, seems to be interested in form and meter. . . .[4]

Wojahn is describing with clinical accuracy the situation which, as an aspiring poet, I remember facing as an undergraduate, the moment before the start of what was to be a "boom" in creative-writing pedagogy in American universities and colleges. As I described that moment years later when introducing William Stafford to a large audience in Topeka:

The poem [Stafford's "Traveling through the Dark"] ran squarely against the dominant style of that time. That style, which has come to be known as "late modernism," was dictated by academics. It was nattering and mannered, produced mainly by genteel scholars, by men who could afford the best dental care, pick out the finest,

low-profile, elbow-patched Harris tweed jackets—by careful, ironic
little men, bureaucrats who, if they put down their copies of Jessie
Weston's *From Ritual to Romance* and ventured outdoors, it would
only be to mow the lawn.

As college and universities expanded to keep pace with demo-
graphic trends, higher education in America became democratized
as it never had been before. The sixties saw a democratization
of poetry (and of high culture in general), the scale of which is
accurately measured by Berry's word "industry." Virtually all the
main trends in poetry during the late sixties and early seventies—
stylistic as well as institutional—can be in part or else entirely
attributable to "democratization." With the establishment of the
National Endowment for the Arts in the late sixties, for the first
time ever in the history of American letters poets could get finan-
cial backing from sources other than conservative English depart-
ments. Starting in the late sixties a whole generation of young
poets, using the fanciful formulas pioneered by Kenneth Koch
and laid out in his book *Wishes, Lies and Dreams*, served as a
sort of domestic Peace Corps in the NEA-funded Poets-in-the-
Schools program—a program which, in an attempt to interest
young people in poetry, encouraged a kind of poetry which could
almost be regarded as "oral-formulaic." But the popularization of
high culture had its cost, most memorably remarked in Jacques
Barzun's infamous and bitter little dictum: "College is a place
where artificial pearls are synthesized for real swine." Poets-in-
the-Schools, while humanizing poetry for children, propagated
the sentimental and inaccurate notion that poetry could become
a body of knowledge available to people who didn't necessarily
read very much or well.

Another of the more notable symptoms of the democratization
of poetry was that, for a while at least, the most prominent American poetry vortices shifted from the coasts—from Boston, New
York, and San Francisco—to the Midwest, revolving around such
figures as Robert Bly and James Wright. Because of the prolif-

eration of creative writing workshops in colleges and universities during the sixties—workshops pioneered at the University of Iowa under the direction of Paul Engle—a vortex that was, in origin, midwestern, spread copies of itself throughout the United States. For the first time ever, American poetry became decentralized, and this decentralization appears to be permanent, at least so long as creative-writing pedagogy is supported by American colleges and universities.

The two most prominent poetic modes that flowered between 1960 and 1976, "confessional" poetry and "deep-image" poetry, were, similarly, part and parcel of American poetry's democratization and industrialization. The kinds of anguished personal experience—divorce, insanity, alienation—which the confessionals wrote about were subjects open to *everybody*, and didn't require research or recondite cultural initiation. Similarly, almost by definition, the "archetypal" dream materials that were the subject matter of poems in the "deep-image" mode not only were ahistorical, but they constituted materials open, literally, to everybody, regardless of intellect, caste, class, education, or geography. Meanwhile, partly because of available funding, but also because of the democratized, *non*literary character of much poetry in the late sixties and early seventies, the institution of the "poetry reading" flourished on college campuses as perhaps it never had before. *Naked Poetry* (1969) was the appropriate title of one of the most prominent anthologies of contemporary poetry of that period, and one of its editors, Stephen Berg, founded *The American Poetry Review*, whose premier issue, featuring David Ignatow, Norman O. Brown, Pablo Neruda, and Denise Levertov, appeared in December 1972 and whose motto was Whitman's optimistic and democratic dictum that for there to be great poets there must be great audiences. *The American Poetry Review* was, from its outset, promoting "open form" poetry, democratization.

Perhaps the final index of the degree of democratization of American poetry was the founding and publication of *Coda* (1973), along with the first issue of *A Directory of American Poets*, both funded by the National Endowment for the Arts. *Coda* made previously "inside" information about poetry contests and publication easily available to everybody in the country.

Since 1976, many of the prominent events, both in the evolution of poetic styles and in the criticism of poetry in America can be considered as elements of a backlash to the liberal democratization of poetry which had, as Berry suggests, been going on since 1964—a reaction signaled most emphatically by Robert Pinsky's book-length critical essay *The Situation of Poetry*, and by the publication of Daniel Halpern's *The American Poetry Anthology*. Both books signaled a set of new and interrelated developments in American poetry. If these developments had any one thing in common it was that they were characterized by an increased self-consciousness about poetic artifice and poetic epistemology, a self-consciousness which, except for M. L. Rosenthal's important study, *The New Poets* (Oxford, 1967), in which the term *confessional poetry* was invented, had been notably absent during the sixties and early seventies; for the very nature of the "confessional" and "deep-image" modes, when they held sway in the late sixties and early seventies, had militated against the self-conscious display of craft or rhetorical calculation. Both Pinsky's book and the poems in the Halpern anthology expressed dissatisfaction with the prevailing poetic decorum and signaled the restoration to respectability of a wide variety of poetic modes which, under the hegemony of Eliot and the New Critics and, later, in the anti-intellectual counterrevolution of the late sixties, had been relegated to a marginal status in the evolving milieu of American poetry.

Although Pinsky's essay was closely reasoned, urbane in its tone and almost scholarly in its rhetoric, without the shrillness of the famous *imagiste* manifestos, it was, in effect, a manifesto. It was overtly opinionated. It chided Robert Bly for a "more-imagistic-than-thou" attitude; and it pointed out, in a tone that was both

troubled and amused, how stock had become the vocabulary of
the "deep-image" poem:

> One of the most contemporary strains in contemporary poetry
> is often interior, submerged, free-playing, elusive, more fresh than
> earnest, more eager to surprise than to tell. The "surrealist" diction
> associated with such writing sometimes suggests, not a realm be-
> yond surface reality, but a *particular* reality, hermetically primitive,
> based on a new poetic diction: "breath," "snow," "future," "blood,"
> "silence," "eats," "water," and most of all "light" doing the wildly
> unexpected. . . . This is a kind of one-of-the-guys surrealism.[5]

Pinsky's main thrust was to remind the reader of the artificiality of poetic conventions, that the apparent spontaneity of
"deep-image" poems and of poems in the romantic tradition was
really a highly evolved period style, a set of mannerisms—that
indeed the very nature of language renders the presentation of
"immediate" experience impossible:

> Modern poetry was created by writers born about a hundred years
> ago. The premises of their work included a mistrust of abstraction
> and statement, a desire to escape the blatantly conventional aspects
> of form, and an ambition to grasp the fluid, absolutely particular
> life of the physical world by using the static, general medium of
> language. These premises are paradoxical, or at least peculiar, in
> themselves. Moreover, the brilliant stylistic inventions associated
> with these premises—notably the techniques of "imagism," which
> convey the powerful illusion that a poet presents, rather than tells
> about, a sensory experience—are also peculiar as techniques.
>
> Or, they once seemed peculiar. These special, perhaps even tor-
> mented premises and ways of writing have become a tradition: a
> climate of implicit expectation and tacit knowledge.[6]

Pinsky's allegation that the poetry he was criticizing was
founded on a fraudulent epistemology was, perhaps, overdrawn;
but his suggested antidote to "imagism" as an exhausted period

style—that poetic language could and should admit more abstract discourse—seemed to prophesy or at least to acknowledge and to ratify trends that were already taking place. Some of these trends could already be discerned among the poems in Halpern's anthology: the "meditative" poetry of a writer like Robert Hass, the narrative realism of poets like Gary Gildner or Frank Bidart, the formalism of a poet like Marilyn Hacker, the wit of a poet like William Matthews, all under forty when the Halpern anthology was published.

Indeed, perhaps the most significant symptom of the increasing self-consciousness among poets and their readers that we observe around 1976 is that this year marks, approximately, the beginning of a large outpouring of excellent practical criticism much like the outpouring that accompanied the advent of "modernism" in 1913. Why such an outburst at this time? Probably because of the very "industrialization" of creative writing that Berry had complained about; for in the dozens of creative writing programs, which had sprung up in imitation of the Iowa Writers Workshop as its graduates spread out like missionaries through American colleges and universities, as American creative writing reached an "industrial" scale, the pressure upon young writers to master or to imitate the period style of the moment grew correspondingly more acute. It grew in direct proportion to the number of competing writers and the degree of the institutionalization of poetry. To attack the dominant mode of the moment was tantamount to attacking an institution.

The most intelligent and telling attack on the outgoing "deep-image" period style was by Paul Breslin, in his essay "How to Read the New Contemporary Poem," published in *The American Scholar* in 1978, an essay which, in a rather more acerbic version, had been delivered by Breslin in 1977 at MLA, under the title "Nihilistic Decorum in Contemporary American Poetry," with its opening complaint that a "narrow and dull decorum" had spread over most American poetry.

An equally important critical survey of contemporary American poetry was Stanley Plumly's two-part essay "Chapter and Verse," published in 1977 in *The American Poetry Review*. During the late sixties and early seventies, in reaction to the genteel, ironic, metered, "late-modernist" poetry of the late fifties—the mode epitomized in the first edition (1957) of *New Poets of England and America*—"free verse" had become virtually the lingua franca of poetic discourse. But it wasn't until Plumly's essay that the prevailing fashion of free verse was given any theoretical justification. Plumly, a highly accomplished poet himself, characterized the typical free-verse poem as a "prose lyric," a type of poem relying on the "rhetoric" of "voice" instead of the "silent" rhetoric of the "image." The primacy of "voice" in Plumly's aesthetic reflected three aspects of the contemporary tradition in 1977: (1) the popularity, already waning but still significant, of the poetry reading, in which the poet's voice was actually present before an audience; (2) the beginning of a shift in fashion, away from the "narrow and dull" deep-image lyric decorum impugned by Breslin, toward a poetic milieu that would tolerate and even encourage a greater diversity of modes, including the narrative—a mode in which the existence of a storytelling "voice" would seem to have always been inherently necessary; (3) a restoration of the dignity of individual personality in poetry. Whereas the Jungian epistemology of "deep-image" poetry had encouraged the cultivation by poets of a generic, archetypal persona speaking for all humanity for all time, the narrative, free verse, conversation poem that was the "prose lyric" had, by definition, to be spoken by a particular individual, from a particular historical moment.

What is perhaps more significant, Plumly's justification for free verse as specially adaptable for individual "voice" comprised the most convincing denial yet formulated for the implicit justification of free verse in "deep-image" poetry, which had assumed that a poetry whose content issued directly from the unconscious could never admit to too much conscious craft and prosodic artifice. "Deep-image" poetry *had* to look spontaneous, primitive, and crude. Plumly's essay was the first attempt by a poet to argue the case for free verse on the grounds of its application toward sophisticated, civilized intentions, on the grounds of its potential *urbanity*. In this respect, Plumly's essay, like Pinsky's *The Situation of Poetry*, was a landmark work, foreshadowing most of the major developments in American poetry that have occurred since 1977.

A more scholarly approach to free verse was Charles O. Hartman's *Free Verse*. Whereas Plumly's "Chapter and Verse" had been of a practical nature, Hartman's approach was both historical and theoretical. Although it adduced some brilliant, detailed demonstrations of the application of free verse, its main thrust was to develop an updated organic theory of poetic form, which Hartman called "discovered" form. What was perhaps most significant about Hartman's approach was that, although he was analyzing a prosody that had flowered as a reaction *against* "late-modernist" genteel versification, his critical rigor, with its concern about "the intentional fallacy" and its aim to propose a *rational* basis for the operations of free verse strongly resembled the earlier New Criticism. In this respect, Hartman's study, more than Plumly's, was reactionary.

In 1990, Hartman's book was rendered obsolete by Timothy Steele's *Missing Measures*, a book which, in its thoroughness and erudition was perhaps the equal of Hugh Kenner's *The Pound Era* and which, in its pellucid style, exceeded Kenner. Steele drew significant links between questions of prosody and questions of genre, presenting modern poetry and its favored prosody of *vers libre* as an anomaly—a well-meaning but short-lived experiment:

> The last two hundred years . . . mark a change. Many of the finest fiction writers of the age compose in prose rather than in meter, and the modern novel acquires a popularity and respectability formerly accorded to epic, verse drama, and lyric. Indeed, by the end of the nineteenth century, the novel is the dominant form of fiction. Modern poets commonly urge that poetry has lost much of its material to prose fiction and that if poetry is to recover that material it must

assimilate characteristics of the novel. Whereas in earlier times prose writers experimented with incorporating verse cadences into prose, poets now begin to experiment with integrating the relative rhythms of prose into verse. Prose becomes, in short, the primary art.[7]

Of the cultural and poetic developments begun in the late sixties and early seventies, only one continued to gain momentum, both critical and creative, after 1976. This was the creation, begun by Adrienne Rich, of a distinct "women's" poetic tradition, a creation signaled by her landmark essay/lecture, "When We Dead Awaken," published first in *College English* (October 1972) and reprinted in William Heyen's anthology, *American Poets in 1976*, but signaled more emphatically by Rich's National Book Award–winning poetry collection *Diving into the Wreck* (1973). It was in 1976, however, that this emerging tradition was given its first thorough critical definition, by the poet/critic Suzanne Juhasz, in her study *Naked and Fiery Forms: Modern American Poetry by Women*. Whereas critical approaches such as Plumly's, Pinsky's, Hartman's, and Steele's were reactionary, Juhasz's study—as revolutionary a manifesto as Pinsky's *The Situation of Poetry* was a conservative one—proposed an aesthetic for what she perceived, accurately as it turns out, to be an emerging women's tradition in American poetry—a tradition availing itself of the spirit of "liberation" that had characterized so much of the political rhetoric of liberals and radicals during the late sixties and the early seventies:

The new tradition exists: wrought slowly through the century with pain and daring, it daily encounters and confronts a growing audience. No one style or form defines it, yet certain qualities do characterize the poetry of contemporary women poets: a voice that is open, intimate, particular, involved, engaged, committed. It is a poetry whose poet speaks as a woman, so that the form of her poem is an extension of herself. A poetry that seeks to affect actively its audience. A poetry that is real, because the voice that speaks is as real as

the poet can be about herself. . . . A poetry that is revolutionary, because, both "naked and fiery," it touches, and [in the words of Nikki
Giovanni] "touching was and still is and will always [be the true]
revolution."[8]

Ten years later, in her short essay "American Poetry Now,
Shaped by Women," Alicia Ostriker would write:

> There is reason to believe that American women poets writing
> in the last 25 years constitute a literary movement comparable to
> Romanticism or modernism in our literary past and that their work is
> destined not only to enter the mainstream but to change the stream's
> future course. To be sure, the idea of "women's poetry" is still dis-
> tressing in some quarters, as is the whole notion of a female literary
> tradition. Most critics and professors of literature deny that women's
> poetry, as distinct from poetry by individual women, exists. . . . Yet
> we do not hesitate to use the term "American poetry" (or "French
> poetry" or "Russian poetry") on the grounds that American (or
> French or Russian) poets are diverse. . . . The belief that true poetry
> is genderless—which is a disguised form of believing that true poetry
> is masculine—fails to recognize that writers necessarily articulate
> gendered experience just as they necessarily articulate the spirit of a
> nationality, an age, a language.[9]

Like Juhasz, Ostriker proposed that women's poetry is characterized by its intimate and direct contact with its audience:

> The best women writers tend to be intimate rather than remote,
> passionate rather than distant, and to defy divisions between emotion
> and intellect, private and public, life and art, writer and reader. . . .
> If poetry written by contemporary women demands that we read as
> participants, it may help us discover not only more of what it means
> to be a woman but more of what it means to be human.[10]

Meanwhile, although the sixties were over, the poetry
"industry" in 1976 was still expanding. Associated Writing Programs, founded in 1967 by R. V. Cassill "for the purpose of

(1) Establishing a clearing house to place writers more usefully and profitably in the main stream of literary tradition; (2) Building a new publishing and reading community within the academic community among the academic multitudes; and (3) Supporting and defining the master of fine arts degree as a terminal degree for those whose primary and long-term commitment to letters is a commitment to writing and its relevant disciplines," grew steadily in influence and membership, as it provided guidance to the hundreds of creative writing programs being introduced in colleges and universities. In 1975, AWP instituted its award series book competition in fiction and poetry. By 1984, *The AWP Catalogue of Writing Programs* contained descriptions for 279 writing programs in the United States and Canada.

In Vermont in 1976, the poet Ellen Bryant Voigt had founded, at Goddard College, America's first "limited residency" M.F.A. creative writing program, an innovative pedagogical structure in which, reinforced by two, intensive, twelve-day residencies each year, talented students could, by means of regular exchanges of mail, have their writing critiqued in detail by established writers.

The growth of creative writing pedagogy and the numbers of talented graduates from the burgeoning creative writing programs resulted in the creation of publishing opportunities other than the new AWP Award Series. The Walt Whitman Award, the Princeton Poetry Series, and the Houghton Mifflin Poetry Series were all instituted in 1976; and 1968 saw the founding of the Pitt Poetry Series and The Elliston Award (for the best collection published by a small press). In the September/October 1977 issue of *Coda*, a headline reported, with some alarm: "Editors deluged by submissions." In 1979, with the help of a massive grant by the author James Michener and the administrative skill of the poet/editor Daniel Halpern, The National Poetry Series was instituted. By the mid-1980s, probably more good poetry was being written and published in America than in any country at any time in human history. Indeed, America was perhaps the only country in history in which hundreds of people could earn a living as poets, teaching creative writing in universities at a professor's salary while travel-ing regularly to give poetry readings at other universities. Not only was the quality of much of this poetry very high, but, for rea-sons I have already suggested, the kinds of poems being written and published were various, constituting an aesthetic pluralism.

Although the drift of American poetry has been in a conservative direction, its main and central strand has been its "realist" component, continuing the liberal, humanistic, and egali-tarian cultural projects of the late sixties and early seventies. Within this strand, the now fully emerged "women's" poetic tra-dition has been the most vital. The reason for this is simple. Realism, as a glance at the work of such American early mod-ern classics as *Babbitt* and *Winesburg, Ohio* would suggest, has always derived its impetus and force from the act of exposure of uncomfortable and inadequately acknowledged truths underlying various forms of official complacency. This is why, for the last fif-teen years, virtually all of the important realist fiction in America has been written by women. Whereas except when writing about odd corners of experience such as the Vietnam War, male fiction writers in America, lacking material crying for exposure, have had to content themselves largely with fabulation and formal ex-periment, the details of life as a female in America had never been, until recently, thoroughly scrutinized from a female point of view.

The dichotomy between men's and women's writing, glaring in the domain of serious fiction, is also apparent, in slightly dif-ferent form, in the differences that have evolved between male and female poetry in America. Although "realistic" in setting and characterization, much American male poetry tends to be what Wendell Berry labeled a poetry of "sensibility." Much female poetry, on the other hand, though often anguished and passionate, attempts to deal realistically with questions of history, ideology, social and personal responsibility—to deal with ideas rather than "feelings" in an attempt to reveal, almost analytically, connec-tions between the subjective life of an individual female and the

objective political, economic, and personal facts that determine
her situation. Paradigmatic of this type of poetry at its best might
be Sharon Olds's important collection, *The Dead and the Living*,
published by Knopf, a book that was both the Lamont Poetry
Selection for 1983 and a National Book Critics Circle Award winner. The confessional poems that comprise the strongest half of the
book, poems replete with gritty journalistic detail, expose almost
relentlessly the links between Olds's ostensibly safe, comfortable
bourgeois life as a mother, on the one hand, and various unpleas-
ant historical facts—the holocaust, wars waged by male govern-
ments, imperialism, and oppression—on the other. The book is
energized by Olds's agonized sense of responsibility at her *female*
role as a bearer of children into a world in which, all too easily,
they could find themselves either being victims or oppressors. By
alternating between public events and poems about domestic, private life, Olds dramatizes how her own body—exemplary of the
female body in its potentiality for birth—is located at the very
nexus of history, of past and future, of public and private, of the
dead and of the living, how as a mother one is drawn not just
theoretically into history but into it *bodily*—that there is no shel-
ter from it or from one's responsibility in it. Thus, in "Rite of
Passage," Olds is able to be horrified by her own son as a first
grader:

> As the guests arrive at my son's party
> they gather in the living room—
> short men in first grade
>
> .   .   .   .
>   They clear their
> throats a lot, a room of small bankers,
> they fold their arms and frown. *I could beat you*
> *up,* a seven says to a six,
>
> .   .   .   .
> *We could easily kill a two year old,*
> he [Olds's son] says in his clear voice. The other

men agree, they clear their throats
like Generals, they relax and get down to
playing war, celebrating my son's life.[11]

This insistence on exploring the nature and degree of one's responsibility to the world and one's personal and historical connections with it supplies the driving impulse behind the work of two other very important American women poets writing today: Carolyn Forché, whose *The Country Between Us* tries to repair the disrelation between felt individual life in America and American oppression in Central America; and Carolyn Kizer, whose *Yin*, winner of the 1985 Pulitzer Prize, forges a passionate female mythology in which marriage, children, and generational continuity are celebrated. Two of the most ambitious poems in *Yin*, "The Copulating Gods" and "Semele Recycled," propose, in complementary ways, a modern mythology of gender. "The Copulating Gods," assuming the sexual superiority of women to men, portrays human religion and poetry as issuing from an eternal female principle so powerful and pervasive that it drives males to invent compensatory male sky gods such as Jupiter. God, who is female, thus allows both herself and her poems to be reinvented in male manifestations, by men, and explicated by male "theologians," male critics. The poem is in the form of pillow-talk, spoken by a goddess to her divine boyfriend (Apollo?): "We" signifies females, "gods," poets: poet is to critic as god (female) is to human (male):

> Come, kiss!
> Come, swoon again, we who invented dying
> And the whole alchemy of resurrection.
> They will concoct a scripture explaining this.[12]

The poem's vision of the complementarity and mutual dependence of "male" and "female" is more than a joke or some clever paradox: it is the most lyric and yet rigorously developed proposal of how both genders may accommodate one another that any contemporary poet, including Adrienne Rich, has put forth. The mythology that Kizer is proposing is elaborated further in "Semele Recycled," a poem which, while describing with moving authenticity, in terms of the legend of Semele, the ways in which males may sexually use females and leave them "broken into pieces," ends on a profoundly affirmative note. The female principle, by nature, resurrects itself. It is at the root of the life-force in both the human and the inhuman domains:

> And here it is, moonlight again; we've bathed in the river
> and are sweet and wholesome once more.
> We kneel side by side in the sand;
> we worship each other in whispers.
> But the inner parts remember fermenting hay,
> the comfortable odor of dung, the animal incense,
> its birth and rebirth and decay.[13]

In American *male* poetry in the 1980s, the most vital strand of the new "realism" has, like poetry in the women's tradition, derived its impetus from acts of exposure—exposure not of veiled truths about gender and power but of the hidden costs of middle-class comfort in American society. Philip Levine had been publishing such poems for years—poems evincing explicitly a political/social conscience in a historical context—but, perhaps as a reaction against the oddly fraudulent opulence of American middle-class life in the 1980s, as if America were reenacting one hundred years later a "gilded age" political style—a number of American poets younger than Levine were writing poems that eloquently took up the task of exposure. Foremost among these poets has been C. K. Williams, in whose strongest collection, *Tar*, the poems try, repeatedly, to come to terms with disturbing social and economic facts, with the question of how, if one is a reasonably prosperous and secure member of the middle class in America at this historical moment, one can reconcile one's comfort and prerogatives with the blatant suffering and exploitation that immediately surround one, with a discrepancy between privileged and poor which, especially in cities like Newark, N.J. (where most of Williams's poems are set), the Reagan administration's policies enlarged to glaring proportions during the early eighties.

The vast majority of male American realism, however, has not been political but has been, as is the nature of much realism, regional, a poetry of local color: Sydney Lea writing about New Hampshire, Brendan Galvin writing about Cape Cod, Stephen Dunn and Louis Simpson writing about eastern suburban life, Ted Kooser writing about small-town Nebraska life, the late Richard Hugo (1923–82) writing about Montana and the Pacific Northwest, Philip Booth writing out of the severity of Maine, Philip Schultz in *Deep in the Ravine* capturing the daily nightmare of felt life in New York City, Jared Carter and David Etter telling stories of middle-American life.

Galvin and Hugo represent rural, local-color regionalism at its best. They celebrate, through rich description, vanishing ways of life, ways of life that in America are being all but obliterated by housing developments, malls, and freeways. The more marginal such local cultures become, the more elegiacally they are celebrated. Galvin's celebration of the lives of Cape Cod fishermen or of the eighteenth-century naturalist "Loranzo Newcomb," Hugo's celebration of the backward lives in economically depressed, dilapidated, western towns bypassed by freeways, are examples of a nostalgic thematic that came into prominence in English language poetry with Wordsworth and that would appear to constitute an inevitable by-product of the development of industrial and postindustrial society.

As might be expected, however, the geographical region richest in local color has remained the South. The most influential realist, writing in the tradition of America's first official poet laureate, Robert Penn Warren, has proved to be Dave Smith, whose ancestral ground is the tidewater region of Virginia. *The Roundhouse Voices*, Smith's new and selected poems, published by Harper and Row in 1986, is deeply and authentically southern—Faulknerian in its oral quality of being a layered assemblage of stories told by a medley of voices who together comprise an insistent, sad, stubborn gossip issuing from the mind not so much of a single individual as a place, a mythic community. As Smith writes in "The Colors of Our Age: Pink and Black":

> Out here, supper waiting, I watch my son
> slip off, jacketed, time, place,
> ancestors of no consequence to him,
>
> . . . .
>
> For him, we are the irrelevance of age.
> Who, then, will tell him of wars,
> of faces that gather in his face
> like shadows? [14]

The most strident publication backing realism and, as an aspect of "realism" narrative poetry, was a little magazine called *The Reaper*, started in 1981 by Robert McDowell and Mark Jarman, at Indiana State University, Evansville. *Reaper I* introduced itself with a manifesto that proclaimed:

> Navel gazers and mannerists, their time is running out. Their poems, too long even when they are short, full of embarrassing lines that "context" is supposed to justify, confirm the suspicion that our poets just aren't listening to their language anymore. . . . inaccuracy, bathos, sentimentality, posturing, evasion—wither at the sound of *The Reaper*'s whetstone singing. . . . The poems collected here in issue number one, unmannered, tell stories *which their imagery serves*.[15]

The Reaper, like Pinsky, was intent on exposing literary manners that had gone stale. Whereas Pinsky's proposed antidote to empty manners was admission into poetic discourse of more abstract statement, *The Reaper*'s antidote was more narration. Narrative could serve as a reminder to poets that in order to make a good poem one must have a valid occasion to write about, an occasion urgent enough and dramatic enough to be the springboard for a story.

The poet whom *The Reaper* showcased as exemplary of the

power of narrative was Jared Carter, whose poems such as "The Gleaner" and "The Shriving" transplanted to a midwestern setting verse stories that were altogether the equal of early Frost poems. Meanwhile, other poets, perhaps out of weariness with lyric decorum, with its narrow focus on the poet's "inner life" and with what Wendell Berry had called its "estrangement from story telling," began to experiment with narration. Louis Simpson adopted an urbane, omniscient, Chekhovian storytelling voice in order to write, in verse, stories about characters other than himself. Perhaps the most celebrated storyteller in the later 1980s, however, was C. K. Williams. In poems such as "Tar" and "The Gas Station," Williams invented a long poetic line that enabled him to speak poems in a storytelling voice, to incorporate all the digressions necessary in artful storytelling while retaining some of the relentless forward movement and intensity of lyric.

Realism is perhaps by nature democratic and egalitarian —*low* mimetic (my emphasis) to borrow Northrop Frye's useful distinction, and in the 1980s American realism in poetry has been, in every sense, "middle of the road." Its formal characteristics—free verse, vernacular diction—are natural to it. They evolved almost inevitably from Whitman. The two most recent main developments in American poetry have diverged in opposite directions from the dominant "centrist" position of realism, one toward the political right, one toward the political left. Of the two, the most prominent has been, as I have already suggested, reactionary, and has manifested itself mainly in the formulation of a conservative poetic style that has come to be known as "The New Formalism." The other main development, "Language Poetry," is radical, using literary and also High-Theoretical Criticism as a springboard for the criticism of bourgeois, "capitalist" culture. Like the political Left itself, this style is a marginal one. As these two styles, New Formalism and Language poetry, developed in the early eighties, it was as if their differences reflected divisions evolving in the socioeconomic fabric of America itself under the Reagan administration.

The New Formalism accomplished the partial gentrification of American poetry, as the latest members of the old elite—the genteel interests which, in the late fifties, in the height of Eliot's hegemony, had guided the tradition—attempted to get back what had been theirs. Symptomatic of this restoration of the old system of influence might, perhaps, be the assumption of James Merrill to the office of judge for the Yale Younger Poets Series, in 1983, replacing Richard Hugo. The literary journal created by Hilton Kramer as the main publishing organ of the New Formalism, *The New Criterion*, by appropriating the name of the famous journal once edited by T. S. Eliot, very pointedly allied itself with Eliot's conservative, "Tory" values.

"The New Formalism" retrieved the strand of ironic, fixed-form, "late-modernist" poetry, which had reigned briefly in the late fifties, a strand epitomized, perhaps, by the vintage work of Richard Wilbur. But whereas "late-modernist" poetry, conceived under the spell of Eliot and influenced heavily by Eliot's rediscovery of the English metaphysicals, had been "metaphysical" itself—constructed around philosophical paradoxes and employing extended metaphors whose legitimacy derived from comparison to metaphysical conceits—the poems of the first "New Formalist" poet to gain a reputation, Brad Leithauser, dealt with such issues as the poet's adjustment to the practice of law, the social and sexual dynamics of tennis classes. It seemed to be poetry by the rich, about the minor worries of the rich, a sort of expensive, very tasteful, interior decoration. Richard Wilbur had given formalism its most memorable dictum in his famous metaphor, which held that rhyme and meter were necessary in order to contain the pent-up energy of content in the same sense that the power of a "genie" was derived from the pressure of its captivity in a bottle. The New Formalism, as practiced by Leithauser, produced elegant bottles without genies in them, or, as Leithauser characterized the sonnet in his essay "Metrical Illiteracy," "robust little music box[es]." In "'Yes, But' . . . ," Wojahn, analyzing Leithauser's "Law Clerk, 1979," concluded that "the satire does little more than to reveal the speaker's mean spiritedness and shoddy elitism."

Much as the early modernist movement had, with Pound's cry to compose "not in the sequence of a metronome," the New Formalism (like that "movement" known as the "new narrative") advertised itself by means of the word "new" as one side in a polemic. Some of the theorizing that the New Formalists employed to support their position was ingenious. Perhaps the most ingenious was Frederick Turner's and Ernst Poppel's essay "The Neural Lyre," which justified iambic pentameter by offering scientific proof that "The average number of syllables per LINE in human poetry seems to be about ten" and takes approximately three seconds to hear, as if such a justification were needed. But except for Timothy Steele's book *Missing Measures*, the New Formalists' programs—Leithauser's essay "Metrical Illiteracy," for example, or the Introduction by Frederick Turner and Frederick Feirstein to their collection *Expansive Poetry: Essays on The New Narrative and The New Formalism*—were ineptly presented. Leithauser's tone resembled that of a rather pedantic English don:

> The willing reader . . . is offered *disturbing collections,* and *disturbing new voices* . . . the books themselves are apt to prove not so much *disturbing* . . . as simply *dismaying.* . . .[16]

The essay ends:

> metrical illiteracy is, for the poet, functional illiteracy. To write a competent Miltonic sonnet— . . . one which satisfies formal requirements without relying on padding or wrenched syntax . . . is a surprisingly difficult undertaking. Surely all poets ought to know this, even if not all critics do.[17]

The tone of the Introduction to *Expansive Poetry* bordered on hysteria:

> It is hard to imagine in 1989 how narrow and doctrinaire was the world of poetry in the seventies when the poets in the movement began to mature. Both narrative and meter were considered at best out of date and at worst the instruments of bourgeois capitalism. . . . the high priests of the ruling ideology proclaimed that narrative and

meter were elitist European importations and that the true American voice could only be heard in "free verse." A socio-economic structure involving a peculiar collusion of interests between the poets themselves, the grant-giving organizations such as the National Endowment for the Arts, the academic creative writing workshops, the small magazines and presses, helped to preserve this conception of the role and nature of poetry. . . . The academy was both the villain and the theatre of the poetic act. . . . Some of us quit teaching. In the poetry world itself our "experimenting" with form and narrative led us to become very uncomfortably isolated, even scorned. . . . we were as isolated in the poetry world as we'd been in society at the end of Gray Flannel culture. We even began to feel the poetry world itself was just another county in the wasteland of television.[18]

The exaggerations of the *Expansive* "manifesto" were gratuitous. Not only had "formalism" never been "new" (such poets as Judith Moffett, Marilyn Hacker, Fred Chappell, Richard Moore, and Lewis Turco had been working in forms for years), but except for Wilbur and James Merrill, most of the American poets who in 1957 had been featured in *New Poets of England and America* and had demonstrated in that anthology their mastery of the forms had later chosen to work, with greater success, in free verse. The subtext of *Expansive Poetry* was not aesthetic but political. It arose apparently from the editors' feeling of being outsiders—a jealousy that was puzzling, since by 1989 the editors had been duly recognized, both inside and outside the academy.

One of the most spectacular productions of the New Formalists was an entire novel (307 pages) in verse, *The Golden Gate*, by Vikram Seth, published in 1986 by Random House. Reviewing it in the *Los Angeles Times*, the poet X. J. Kennedy, who from 1972 to 1974 had edited the journal *Counter/Measures: A Magazine of Rime, Meter and Song*, wrote:

> A novel about the manners and morals of Silicon Valley yuppies might well be expected to make at least a local stir, but why all this coast-to-coast hullabaloo? The answer is clear: It isn't merely

Mr. Seth's revelations of yuppiedom. Awe strikes whoever casts a glance up this mountain of technical virtuosity. *The Golden Gate*— all of it, even its table of contents, its dedication, its autobiographical notes—is written in verse: 593 repeated stanzas, strictly measured and rhymed.[19]

Meanwhile, Harper and Row published a new anthology, edited by Philip Dacey and David Jauss, entitled *Strong Measures: Contemporary American Poetry in Traditional Forms*. By the early 1990s, the New Formalism had indeed grown into a full-fledged institution, with its own journal, its own anthology, and, in Timothy Steele's *Missing Measures*, the most persuasive possible manifesto—a 340-page scholarly repudiation of the aesthetics and the epistemology of modernist poetry.

The corresponding developments on the Left were analyzed in the first issue of *The Reaper*, in a short essay entitled "Navigating the Flood." The essay began:

> In November, 1979, *The Reaper* attended After the Flood, a symposium at the Folger Shakespeare Library in Washington D.C. where panelists Harold Bloom, Richard Howard, John Hollander, Donald Davie, Marjorie Perloff and Stanley Plumly scrutinized the state of contemporary American poetry and its criticism. During the presentation, group discussions and informal chats, the dominant emerging perspective seemed *not* to include the poem, but only ways of talking about the poem. . . . John Hollander implied that a poem in its very form is a critical text that comments on itself. And Harold Bloom typified the symposium's spirit by quoting and misreading, Oscar Wilde: "*The only civilized form of autobiography*—I know no more adequate characterization of the highest criticism." It was remarkable to discover how little the panelists actually disagreed. Since then *The Reaper* has come to a few conclusions about the symposium topic. 1. Poetry, more than ever, is harnessed by and subordinate to its criticism. . . . 3. Critics are creating an exclusive audience for poetry, which consists only of themselves and the poets they promote. . . .

4. When critics cease with explanations and turn to examples, more often than not what they like is not good: they try to invent surprises where no surprise exists. . . . At the symposium, Ashbery was the one poet deferred to, analyzed, airbrushed, fawned over, and lovingly chided by every panelist. . . . However, as became clear at the symposium, contemporary critics are not satisfied with their role. . . . *The Reaper*'s third conclusion is linked to the first and is illustrated by the critics' desire to celebrate the activity of talking about poems—not the art itself. Bloom's theory that a poem, in order to last, must provoke several strong misreadings is a brilliant though diabolical excuse for the perpetuity of criticism, for its domination over poetry. It is a theory that misses the immediate event of the poem itself and implies that the reader cannot know which poems are significant until the critic informs him.[20]

The Reaper's report then went on to detail the response of the symposium to two poems that comprise a type of poem which has come to be called "meditative": "Wet Casements," by John Ashbery, and Robert Hass's "Meditation at Lagunitas," poems which, as if following the directive by Robert Pinsky in *The Situation of Poetry* for admission of more abstract discourse into poems— more "telling" and less "showing"—abandon the imagistic tactics of the lyric in favor of discursive abstract speculation. *The Reaper* suggests that these poems were written, in effect, for critics:

> the critic who is interested primarily in developing a new program for reading can always babble on from the cloying camp of pre-digested theories. What counts is the evasive text which gives the critic the opportunity to invent substance where little exists. Poets who practice this sort of writing hide in their work and lend themselves to abstract theorization.[21]

The Reaper essay concluded:

> Poetry must be written that casts a cold eye on criticism. . . . Are the poems extolled by critics like Harold Bloom, Richard Howard, Stanley Plumly, et al., good poems, or merely grist for critical mills?

Poetry and criticism are two different things. It is time to remember that the poem comes first.[22]

It is now more than ten years since the symposium and eight years since the *Reaper* essay was published, and that essay has proved prophetic. Ashbery is perhaps the most critically acclaimed poet of our moment, and Hass is perhaps the most critically acclaimed poet of the generation following Ashbery. Wallace Stevens, whose meditative later poems are models for Ashbery and Hass, has replaced Eliot at the head of the modernist canon; and various strands of High-Theoretical criticism—reader-response theory and Derridean theory, with their "suspicious" approaches to interpretation of texts—have replaced the old New Criticism. Like the New Criticism, these newer approaches have developed their own specialized jargon and place heavy emphasis upon close reading of "texts"; but unlike the New Criticism, they have refused to take for granted any reliable relation between words and what they might signify. Stevens's approach to language—his poetic demonstrations of the ways in which language predetermines how we view the world instead of describing already known phenomena—has turned out to be almost tailor-made for critics interested in applying fashionable Theory to current poetry. Thus, in a critical study of Wallace Stevens and William Carlos Williams, *The Transparent Lyric*, the critic David Walker was able to propose that the protagonist of many of the poems of Stevens and Williams is not the "speaker" of their poems but the reader: "I propose to call this kind of poem the transparent lyric: in replacing the lyric speaker with the reader as the center of dramatic attention, the poem itself becomes a transparent medium through which the reader is led to see the world in a particular way." Later, Walker writes:

> The transparent lyric may be defined as a poem whose rhetoric establishes its own incompleteness; it is present not as completed discourse but as a structure that invites the reader to project himself or herself into its world, and thus to verify it as contiguous with reality.

In imitating the process of thinking, of confronting the world and responding to it, the poem engages the reader in a different way from poetry grounded in an expressive theory of art, and thus requires a different kind of criticism.[23]

Such an aesthetic, proposed here by a *critic* but implicitly imputed to our poets, recapitulates in slightly more precise terms than the *Reaper* essay had the way in which the current critical climate has attempted to empower critical interpretation with some of the prerogatives of the creative artist. Walker offers the interpreter of a text a blank check and a rationale for using the text of a poem for *any* purpose whatever. A poem, in Walker's eyes, is thus apparently a sort of *ur*-text that a critic—the privileged party in literary discourse—can actually complete.

Walker's preceding description of the "transparent lyric" could even more easily apply to the poetry of John Ashbery than to Stevens or to Williams. Ashbery's poetry seems tailor-made for High-Theoretical treatment. Consider, for example, the following treatment by Charles Altieri, in *Self and Sensibility*, of Ashbery's "No Way of Knowing":

> For Ashbery the mind stands toward its own knowing in the con-dition of infinite regressiveness that Derrida shows is the dilemma inherent in trying to know about the language we use in describing our knowledge . . . for Ashbery the problematics of relation are not primarily of sign and signified but of act to other acts as the mind tries to identify secure resting places.[24]

This passage may sound convoluted, but a glance at the Ashbery poem in question makes it apparent that discourse like Altieri's is the only means of approaching Ashbery linguistically. Most Ashbery poems cannot be explicated by traditional, New-Critical techniques.

The assumption of a shift in poetic authority from poets to crit-ics informs Altieri's *Self and Sensibility* at every point. As stated at the end of Altieri's study:

poetry's obligations remain constant, requiring us to hold contemporary poets to the highest standards developed by our cultural heritage. Without such *critical pressure* [my italics] he may hasten a day when that heritage is in fact as irrelevant as it is often claimed to be. For we will no longer recognize ourselves as capable of sharing the desires it cultivates and the powers it provides.[25]

Although the word *it* in the previous sentence is used equivocally, the equivocation appears to be deliberate: *it* can refer to "our cultural heritage" or to "critical pressure" or to both. Altieri's implication is obvious: critics, not poets, are custodians and interpreters for all of us of "our cultural heritage."

This very issue—whether critical discourse is privileged over poetic discourse—is at the heart of Hank Lazer's more recent essay in *The Missouri Review*, "The Crisis in Poetry." Lazer opens his essay with a quotation by Louis Simpson from Simpson's October 18, 1984, address, "What Is a Poet?" delivered at the Eleventh Alabama Symposium:

For twenty years American poets have not discussed the nature of poetry. There has not been the exchange there used to be. . . . perhaps because arguing over poetry seems trivial when we are living under the shadow of nuclear annihilation. Another reason is the ascendency of criticism. If poets do not speak for themselves others will speak for them, and when poets vacated the platform critics rushed to take their place. The poets have been willing to see this happen—they are workers and not given to abstract thinking. They believe that the best literary criticism and the only kind that's likely to last is a poem.[26]

Lazer then reviews a variety of recent critical books about poetry, giving special attention to "Charles Bernstein's essays [*Content's Dream: Essays 1975–1980*, Sun and Moon Press, 1985], for they challenge many current views about style, ideology, reading, and our relationship to language and the production of meaning," and he dismisses such practical criticism as Peter Stitt's: "Stitt proposes at the outset to write good old humanism, with sincerity and respect, and with its attendant hostility to 'theory,' its lack of interest in questions about the nature of language, or representation. . . . For Stitt to convince us of the validity of his position, he needs to offer some consideration of the relation between the poem (or words) and 'the external truth of the world,' the latter, for me, being hard to imagine as existing *apart* from language."[27] Still later, Lazer makes a statement that is especially revealing in the light of the *Reaper* essay: "Thus Altieri may be right to suggest that 'speculative criticism now attracts much of the audience and the energy the last decade devoted to poetry.' "[28]

Lazer's essay must rank as one of the more important essays about contemporary American poetry written in the last ten years, not because he talks about actual poems—he doesn't—but because the essay is as sympathetic and fair-minded an account as we are likely to get of the very abuses of criticism that *The Reaper* had deplored. But the disarming frankness of Lazer's essay—its main strength—is its main weakness, because it exposes so blatantly (though inadvertently) the motivation behind his stance. Both Lazer and Altieri pick on contemporary poetry for its allegedly "diminished" status not because contemporary American poetry is weak—it has never been stronger—but because it is not interested in what *they* are. The most flagrant omission by both of them is any mention of why the issues that so interest them have conventionally been handled most comfortably in prose rather than verse. Should Wittgenstein's *Tractatus* have been set in verse? Or Marx's *Capital?* Or Hegel? Many American poets have read and understood these books. But they have chosen not to apply Continental philosophy or deconstructionist theory to the art of poetic composition, for much the same reason that a good orthopedic surgeon would know better, when playing tennis, than to try (or even want) to analyze the physical mechanics involved in producing each stroke. Poets are, as Simpson so deftly put it, "workers."

A second and more disturbing omission by Lazer—a de facto omission in Altieri's *Self and Sensibility* as well—is that poems are never discussed as if they were about people's lives. Critics such as these would appear to lead lives in which they did *nothing* except read, in which the only experience that meant anything to them was "textual"—the opposite, perhaps, of "good old humanism." In this respect, their approach to poetry has much in common with that of the so-called Language poets, of whom Charles Bernstein himself may be the most provocative theorist/practitioner. As Marjorie Perloff, who has for some years now been America's most faithful and intelligent chronicler of *avant garde* literature, wrote in her essay "The Word As Such: L=A=N=G=U=A=G=E Poetry in the Eighties": "For Olsen and Creeley, 'Form is never more than an extension of content.' For the Language poet, this aphorism becomes: 'Theory is never more than the extension of practice.' "[29]

The premises of Language poetry follow from the assumption that, as Perloff put it: "poetic discourse is . . . not the expression of words of an individual speaking subject, but the creation of that subject by the particular set of discourses (cultural, social, historical) in which he or she functions."[30] In other words, language is prior to experience: the nature of the signifier determines the nature of the signified. Such an assumption is a logical and only a modest step beyond David Walker's assignment of the *reader* the role of protagonist in poetic discourse: if language, as Bernstein argues, "exists in a matrix of social and historical relations that are more significant to the formation of an individual than any personal qualities of the life or voice of the author," then language itself is the "protagonist" not merely of poetic discourse but of *all* discourse; for the assumptions of Language poetry abolish distinctions between genres. As Perloff wrote: ". . . whatever the generic category, the important distinction to be made is not between 'story' and 'prose poem' or 'story' and 'essay' but, as Charles Bernstein points out, between 'different contexts of reading and different readerships' . . . To read such . . . texts as [Lyn] Hejinian's *My Life* or [Lydia] Boris's *Story*, is to become aware of what Language poets call 'the rights of the signifier.' "[31] The Language poetry movement is, thus, politically radical in that one of its aims is to expose, in the words of Bernstein, "the optical illusion of reality in capitalist thought." Like the criticism of Lazer, it bases its authority not on sympathy with but on almost total disaffection from mainstream American life, from (to borrow Simpson's telling analogy) "the workers," whom such critics—"vanguards" of an aesthetic "proletariat"—presume to guide, all in the best interests of our cultural heritage.

Two final and quite recent developments in American poetry are worth noting. The first development, conservative in *every* respect, is concerned not with formal retrieval but with retrieval in the domain of "content": the readmission into the contemporary tradition of permission for poets to be didactic, especially in the area of religion. Poets such as David Hopes (*The Glacier's Daughter*), Scott Cairns (*The Theology of Doubt*), David Craig (*Peter Maurin*), David Citino in his "Sister Mary Appassionata" poems, and Andrew Hudgins (*Saints and Strangers*) are writing an explicitly Christian poetry, which is testing the possibilities of reincorporating Biblical typology into poetry, and testing whether this typology can be presented in a tactful enough way to interest a sophisticated modern reader.

The second, associated with Story Line Press, a spin-off of *The Reaper*'s narrative program and engineered by Robert McDowell, has billed itself as "The New Narrative," and it is attempting to subject the capabilities of genre to the most daring experiments. Thus, for example, Story Line published, in 1989, an entire verse novel (a thriller in the hard-boiled style of Raymond Chandler), *Dead Reckoning*, by Brooks Haxton. Like the "new" formalism, however, the "new" narrative was not "new." All that was new about it was the length of its poems, poems that were challenging explicitly, though unsuccessfully, Steele's assertion that "the novel is the dominant form of fiction."

The mainstream of American poetry, however—what Altieri calls "the dominant mode" and what Bernstein dismisses as "official verse culture"—has continued to be, whether narrative or meditative, in a realist mode that is essentially egalitarian, university-based, and middle-class, and to be written in a free verse that has, by and large, vastly improved since the sixties, evolved into a flexible medley of older prosodies so rich in echoes that it bears out Eliot's famous dictum that "No verse is ever really free." The strong poems that make up this mainstream bear out, also, Louis Simpson's reminder that, for our poets, "the best literary criticism and the only kind that's likely to last is a poem": Patricia Goedicke's great symboliste poem "Mahler in the Living Room," C. K. Williams's "From My Window," Stephen Dunn's "The Routine Things Around the House," Tess Gallagher's "Each Bird Walking," Linda Gregg's "Whole and Without Bless-ing," William Matthews's "In Memory of the Utah Stars," Jorie Graham's "Two Paintings by Gustav Klimt," Brendan Galvin's "Seals in the Inner Harbor," Carolyn Forché's "The Colonel," Sydney Lea's "The Feud," Philip Booth's *Before Sleep*, Sharon Olds's *The Dead and the Living*, Robert Pinsky's "History of My Heart," Philip Schultz's "Deep Within the Ravine," Philip Levine's *A Walk with Tom Jefferson*, Michael Ryan's *God Hunger*, and so on. Ten years after Halpern's anthology, *The Morrow Anthology of Younger American Poets*—a volume that might almost be con-sidered a sequel to the Halpern anthology, because many of the poets featured in the *Morrow* had first appeared in Halpern's book—displayed the depth and strength of the mainstream, "cen-trist," realist mode.

Flanking this mainstream realism there was, on the Right, a small but disproportionately influential elite sympathetic with such modes as the "New Formalism"; and there was, on the Left—bred out of the same boom in higher education that had turned American poetry into an "industry"—a small but well-entrenched, disaffected set not of poet/critics but of "critic/poets," completing the pluralistic milieu that the astute critic, James E. B. Breslin, in his *From Modern to Contemporary*, urbanely referred to in his concluding chapter title as "Our Town."

Although American poetry was, as Epstein accused it of being, university-based and professionalized, it was *not,* as he asserted "hopeless." It was very much alive—more vigorous than at any time in American history. The issue facing poets was not how to get poetry out of the classroom. The university classroom was an appropriate place for it, the main place where books—not just poetry but books of all kinds—were seriously read. The democratization of poetry was a by-product of the democratization of higher education in general, in America. The issue facing poets, most of whom were supported by universities, was how to sustain and, perhaps, even enlarge the franchise of poetry within the university—to maintain its general high quality without reverting to the elitist "difficulty" of the modernists while retrieving some of the didactic, narrative, and discursive subject matter that poets had, during the early modernist period and again during its attenuated recapitulation in the late-modern period, at first almost defiantly (but later, de facto) ceded to prose genres.

The End of Modernism

2

We are witnessing, in the 1990s, the final exhaustion of that poetic which, in American poetry, has come to be called "modernist." This poetic, invented by Eliot and Pound and given its initial and fullest expression in Eliot's essay "Tradition and the Individual Talent," consisted of three main elements. The first of these, Eliot's doctrine of impersonality, was rhetorical. The second, the elitism and intellectuality of Eliot and Pound, was political. The third, Eliot's notion of the subject matter of poetry as consisting of synthetic "art-emotions," was epistemological.

The first was overturned in the late fifties by Ginsberg's "Howl" and Lowell's *Life Studies*, with the resulting rush (almost of relief) by many poets into the confessional mode. The second—the political dimension of the modernist program, which invested poetic authority in a scholarly, tweedy professor figure whose authority was institutional rather than personal—has been, if not repudiated, then drastically revised. Universities have remained the custodians of poetry; but, as confessional poetry would seem to testify, the subject matter of poetry has, like the American university itself, been democratized: such subjects as divorce, insanity, and alcoholism require no special training. The third, the epistemological part of the modernist program, however, persists as a kind of modernist hangover, one epitomized infamously in MacLeish's dictum, "a poem must not mean / but be." This is the most extreme formulation of the persistent modernist notion that in great poetry "form" and "content" are indissoluble, or, as Frost is said to have put it, "poetry" is that which "gets lost in translation."

Most people would, I think, agree with Frost. I do, almost instinctively, until I stop to consider the implications of this notion, whereupon, like many famous pieces of modernist dogma—for example, Pound's call for "Direct treatment of the thing"—it begins to look casuistical. In its portentous epistemology and its claims for the indissolubility of "form" and "content" in true "poetry," the modernist poetic has always seemed deliberately to equivocate in order to privilege poetic language over all other forms of discourse, especially over discourse intended to communicate information, to have a clear, publicly acknowledged purpose. Indeed, the term *equivocate* may be too mild a term to suggest the extremity of the modernist "form is content" dogma; for one could make this claim much more strongly for a business letter, a tax return, or a newspaper story, for any text that successfully carries out some specific purpose for which it was designed.

Consider, for example, the telephone book, a piece of discourse that has no aesthetic pretentions whatsoever but which is entirely functional. In this case—I find it ironic—we see that the virtue of making the "form" of the discourse indissoluble with its "content" has some real force: the form and the content of a phone book are so deeply implicated that if the names in the phone book weren't ordered alphabetically and printed directly opposite the correct numbers, the phone book would be nonsense, which is to say useless. In the case of a phone book, rather than speaking of "form" following "content," it is perhaps more accurate to speak of form following "function."

The implications of this are obvious. The word *content,* which is meaningful in the context of some intention, some function, be-

comes problematical when applied to certain kinds of poems—
especially to poems that are about poetry, about themselves. Most
of the great modernist poems are largely about poetry itself. They
are poetic experiments. As Pound said in "A Retrospect" when
comparing poets to scientists: "The scientist does not expect to be
acclaimed as a great scientist until he has discovered something."
Discovered what, though? Most of the famous modernist poems
such as *The Waste Land* and the *Cantos* practice art for art's sake.
They are addressed almost exclusively to other poets. As Michael
Ryan stated in his essay "Difficulty and Contemporary Poetry":

> Eliot's The Waste Land and Pound's Cantos were written by writers
> who disdained Larkin's "reading public."
>
>   But their disdain was that of the spurned, and it was couched in
> ideas that became the axioms of modernism. Pound's conviction that
> "the public is stupid" . . . is certainly the blunt emotion behind Eliot's
> cool formulation that a poet "must be difficult." [1]

In order to defend a poetry that they knew had very little public content, poets working in the modernist tradition resorted to
equivocation, for example, to such mysterious notions as that
of "organic form" and to such dicta as Creeley's "form is never
more than an extension of content" or Levertov's "form is never
more than the revelation of content." It is, as Ryan's preceding
statement would suggest, highly significant that the form/content
clichés, the "axioms of modernism," always assert their claims
about *poetry* but never about prose, when in fact, as the example
of the phone book might suggest, the clichés have greater force
when applied to functional prose discourse, to language intended
as communication, than to the most refined symboliste poem.

The most familiar and plausible-sounding form of the modernist "form/content" equivocation—one perfected by the French
symbolists, grafted onto English language poetry by Eliot, and in-
voked, still, by a poet/critic as sophisticated as David Young—
is to resort to an analogy between poetry and music. Young, describing one of his own poems, writes:

I keep coming back to the notion of music because I think it's the truest thing to say about the composition of the poem ["October Couplets"]. To call it a pure musical exercise sounds excessive. Some readers will think it has no music whatsoever. But music is what I was after. . . . Doesn't music, when it works, express all we know and feel, and in a way which we are helpless to explain?[2]

To be sure, the "content" of music—its "subject matter"—is, as Young implies, pure "feeling." Moreover, if the music is any good, and it does not have words, then its "form" and "content" *are* identical. The very term *minor key,* for example, suggests a particular, recognizable range of moods. But even in the best song, there is something strangely nonspecific, nonreferential about the emotional "content" of the music. For example, if you didn't know German or the Gospel, Peter's lament in Bach's *Saint Matthew Passion*—one of the most heartrending arias that I know of—could be about almost *anything* that was heartrending. It could be grieving over the death of a loved one. It could be expressing amorous passion. In the context of the libretto, it is an expression of Peter's shame. He is shriveled with remorse for having denied Christ in order to avoid possible persecution. The music, though, is fundamentally *disrelated* to the text. The music is a rhetoric that could be used to dignify, to intensify just about any text, any situation that a composer wished to make poignant. As Timothy Steele wrote in *Missing Measures*:

> poets desiring musicality seek to make poetry "indefinite" in the way that music is indefinite. . . . when certain modern poets seek musicality, their model is customarily instrumental music. These poets want to escape not only from meter, but from the discursive quality of words as words. . . . when the model is not purely instrumental, it is Wagnerian, in the sense that music dominates the words.[3]

This suggests why, for apologists of symboliste and hermetic poetry, the word *content* is such a useful term. When they speak of the "content" of poetry as being like that of music (i.e., feeling), they don't have to be specific. They don't have to be accountable. They employ the analogy between poetry and music as an evasion. It's a clever one, because it provides the poet with a rationale for not communicating. As Young put it: "Doesn't music, when it works, express all we know and feel . . . ?" Young's question is framed as a rhetorical one, as if the answer were self-evident: yes. But the obvious answer is no, and even if it were yes, the "content" of "all we know and feel" (though Young's phrase "all we know" has a public ring to it) would be almost entirely private, subjective. It would be incommunicable, untranslatable.

Communication, however, has never been part of the modernist program. As Young wrote in his essay "Language: The Poet as Master and Servant":

> personal sincerity . . . and playing around with ideas, are no *substitute* for the heightened and magical command of language that characterizes good poetry. Neither, for that matter, are moral earnestness, political commitment, theological concern, or frankness about one's sex life. Any of these elements may serve to enhance a poem, but that is not the same as saying that they can be equivalent to the sound, movement, energy and economy that language ought to have in poetry.
>
> [Ammons and Wakoski] . . . share, it seems to me, a fatal discursiveness. . . . If I had to find a phrase to characterize the work of these two writers, I would call them "verse essayists" in order to distinguish their use of language from the language of lyric poetry. . . . Perhaps the verse essay is a respectable and legitimate genre, but I wish it wouldn't be confused with lyric poetry. . . .[4]

It is a little shocking to hear a highly intelligent man talking about subject matter as something that, like a touch of some exotic seasoning, might "serve to enhance a poem." Young has things backwards. It is the "sound, movement, energy and economy that language ought to have in poetry" that should serve to "enhance" subject matter. But Young's taste here carries on faithfully the tra-

dition of modernism. As Annie Dillard wrote in 1983 in her essay
"The Purification of Poetry—Right Out of the Ballpark":

> Generally the triumph of the modern in poetry is identical to the tri-
> umph of the lyric as form. . . . The lyric . . . has always made up in
> surface pleasures what it lacked in breadth and depth.[5]

Dillard then traces the modernist lyric back to the French symbolists and Valery, and she says: "Poetry's role was exalted; it
could keep itself pure by a 'refusal to describe.' Poetry, then,
was language purified; its subject matter was poetry."[6] Young,
of course, does not go quite this far; but the modernist preoccu-
pation with what Dillard calls "surface pleasures" is echoed in
Young's praise of the "sound, movement, energy and economy
that language ought to have in poetry." Although Young would
certainly stop short of Valery's "refusal to describe," he would
have poetry purified of ideas, of "fatal discursiveness" if not of
objects in the world. He takes pains to remind us that a "verse
essay" is *not* "lyric poetry," by which he means, I think, "poetry"
as opposed to prose. What Young dismisses as the "verse essay"
is, apparently, prose, set as verse. The distance of Young's position from that of Poe's "Philosophy of Composition" and from
that of the French symbolists is not very great, though Young's
position is a slight improvement. But on the question of whether a
lyric poem can have paraphrasable, translatable meaning, Young
remains intractably modernist. Such meaning is "fatal." Why?

As George Watson stated in *The American Scholar*, in an essay
entitled "The Phantom Ghost of Modernism":

> By the 1920s and after, Eliot's formulations of the principle of un-
> translatability make it clear that it was understood in some absolute
> and unnegotiable sense. "It is a commonplace," he remarked in a late
> lecture of 1942, "to observe that the meaning of a poem may wholly
> escape paraphrase." With that "wholly" Eliot apparently spurned any
> prospect of compromise—the hopeful notion, for example, that a
> paraphrase might be helpful but not sufficient.[7]

Watson then observes that the doctrine of untranslatability is a strategy based upon self-interest:

> If meaning can "wholly" escape paraphrase, as Eliot said, then there can be no point in asking for a paraphrase or in venturing one's own. Modernism cannot be interrogated then; it can only be swallowed whole, much as the cult members of the Moonies swallow the claims of their church.[8]

How much of the alleged inviolability of the "heightened and magical" aspect of the language of lyric is Young willing to compromise? Virtually none. As Watson's preceding remarks suggest, the absolute privileging of untranslatable lyric discourse over all other forms of discourse is the one thing that poets and critics schooled in the modernist poetic cannot bear to give up. The way in which Young ends up defending this lyric privilege is, like all the arguments supporting the modernist poetic, evasive.

In his essay "The Bite of the Muskrat," published in *A Field Guide to Contemporary Poetry and Poetics*, David Young advanced as a model of good poetry the following short lyric by William Stafford:

CEREMONY

On the third finger of my left hand
under the bank of the Ninnescah
a muskrat whirled and bit to the bone.
The mangled hand made the water red.

That was something the ocean would remember:
I saw me in the current, flowing through the land,
rolling, touching roots, the world incarnadined,
and the river richer by a kind of marriage.

While in the woods an owl started quavering
with drops like tears I raised my arm.

Under the bank a muskrat was trembling
with meaning my hand would wear forever.

In that river my blood flowed on.

Of this poem, Young wrote:

> My feeling about Stafford's poem is that its best moments surprised
> him. . . . A good poem is not a bundle of devices that add up to
> literature, but an unerring trajectory into insight, . . . a good poem
> transcends its author's intention and understanding, while a bad
> poem is under its overconfident author's control, alas, at every point.[9]

Everything Young says is right, except that he sidesteps one crucial question: What *is* the "insight" at the end of the poem's
"trajectory?" Either it does not exist at all, or else it is beyond
paraphrase. For me, it does not exist. "Ceremony" is one of the
very few of Stafford's poems that leave me cold. Young, on the
other hand, evidently derives a significant *frisson* from it. What he
terms (inaccurately, I think) "insight" is nothing other than what
we think of as an "effect." Like all such unparaphrasable, symboliste effects, like the famous one produced by Robert Burns's lines,
"The wan moon is setting behind the white wave, / And Time is
setting with me, oh." (an effect that Yeats called "too subtle for the
intellect" and labeled "symbolic writing"), such effects, when they
"work," must remain subjective, incommunicable. Moreover, the
"effect" produced by "Ceremony" (*if* it produces one) is mainly
literary, an Eliotian "art-emotion"—an effect of such artificiality
and refinement that in order to receive it at all one would have to
have undergone extensive pedagogical indoctrination. As Watson
puts it with wicked accuracy: "it can only be swallowed whole."
Charles Altieri in *Self and Sensibility in Contemporary American
Poetry* makes a similar complaint about "Ceremony," that "its
naturalness is literary and its literaryness ultimately so evasive and
self-protective."

"Ceremony" is, of course, not at all typical of Stafford's poetry,

let alone his best poetry, a poetry which, despite Stafford's subtlety and daunting intellect, is genuinely communal in its aims and
has a following that might almost be termed "popular." "Ceremony" is, however, the model that Altieri chooses to illustrate the
prevailing period style (Altieri calls it the "dominant mode") of
American poetry in the early eighties, a mode which, in his words:

> places a reticent, plain-speaking and self-reflective speaker within
> a narratively presented scene evoking a sense of loss. Then the poet
> tries to resolve the loss in a moment of emotional poignance or wry
> acceptance that renders the entire lyric event an evocative metaphor
> for some general sense of mystery about the human condition.[10]

Altieri is exactly right, and in his phrase "a moment of emotional poignance"—a moment that is, implicitly, untranslatable—
he identifies the lingering modernist trait that characterizes much
(but not all) poetry in "the dominant mode." The trait inheres in
the poem's epistemology. "Ceremony" has shucked most of the
other elitist modernist baggage that poets and critics lugged into
the fifties. It is intimate rather than impersonal. It is humble and
plainspoken rather than academic. But, beyond the fact that it
renders a naturalistic scene, it has little public subject matter. It
doesn't hazard, directly or indirectly, any kind of a statement beyond something like "Wow!" ("I saw me in the current!") This is
a significant limitation of much poetry in "the dominant mode."
Unless our poetry can do more than say "Wow!" (or "Ow!"), it is
going to remain of interest mainly to specialists.

It is possible, however, even in "the dominant mode," to make
lyrics that exhibit the surface charm that Young, quite rightly,
insists upon, but that also manage to make profound, subtle, yet
publicly accessible statements. This is the direction in which inevitably American poetry will develop, because the possibilities
of formal innovation are, at this historical moment, drastically
limited. Go back and, like the so-called new formalists, warm
over the late-modernist style of the fifties? No, the changes in

American poetry will be in the domain of "subject matter," of "content," not of "form"; and one could, I think, almost predict what this subject matter will be. It will consist of the very material that David Young says pertains to what he dismisses as the "verse essay": "discursiveness," stories and ideas, many of them explicitly moral and theological—in sum, didactic subject matter, together with imaginative rhetorical tactics to give this material dramatic force, without being preachy or pedantic. A few of our poets such as Wendell Berry, Gary Snyder, Adrienne Rich, William Stafford, Philip Levine, and Allen Ginsberg—poets who (surely it's no accident) have acquired some popular following by nonspecialists—have managed to write great poems that contain some of the broad, "nonliterary" subject matter which, since the modernist movement, American poetry had tended to shun. How to continue this—how to invent rhetorical tactics that might help American poets both to delight *and* instruct an audience other than that of an English department—that is the challenge facing poets at this historical moment. As an example of how one poet has risen to it and of the kinds of rhetorical invention necessary, consider the following poem by Scott Cairns:

HARBOR SEALS

Kill them
if you want to, say, if you're
a fisherman and you think
seals are too good
at catching the fish *you* want,
fish that put food on your family's table.
That's pretty good reasoning. All you need
is a small rifle
and one good eye. Just be sure
you do it quick. It's embarrassing enough
to come across a dead one on the beach,
it's worse to come across one dying.

The one I found had little more
than a scratch across the back of its neck
that sent a dark line of blood
into the sand. A seal's eyes are liquid anyway,
and alert right to the end. When the sea mist
is fine and constant, a seal
can stay beached for hours without
drying out. You don't have to believe
any of this. I sat down close to the idiot
thing, and waited with it for the tide.[11]

This is what I would call a "didactic" poem, one that owes a
great deal to the Christian existentialist writings of Kierkegaard.
The kinds of artistic discovery it makes are rather different from
the kind of free-associational aesthetic "moments" that Young
says, rightly, "surprise" a writer. What it discovers it arrives at
more deliberately than that, and the discovery is more comprehensive. It discovers an entire method for how to teach a difficult,
morally and philosophically charged subject matter. It discovers
a rhetorical tactic for presenting Kierkegaardian ideas without
sounding either doctrinal or gloomy. Instead, it charms the reader,
even as it tempts the reader into a corner, into a rhetorical trap of
bad faith that will require the reader to make a moral choice as
well as to reconsider many other kinds of choices about what to
"believe." Belief—in God, in any kind of moral stance—is a matter of free choice: the poem cheerfully, without sounding cranky,
preachy, or complaining, tells us this over and over again—"Kill
them / if you want to. . . . You don't have to believe / any of
this." In a friendly, almost compassionate tone, Cairns invites us
hypothetical killers to imagine all the best possible excuses with
which we might dismiss the adventitious wounding of a harbor
seal. Perhaps the seal was shot by a frustrated fisherman who was
not catching enough fish to make a living. "That's pretty good
reasoning," Cairns says. He can understand how, in order to rationalize to oneself shooting a harbor seal with a rifle aimlessly,

for sport, one might concoct the plausible sounding argument that harbor seals were significant competitors with us for fish. But this argument could only be made by somebody with "one good eye." Literally, in order to sight along a rifle, you close one eye. Figuratively, if you dismiss the murder and its implications, your vision is one-eyed, without perspective, in that: (1) the rationalization that seals, by catching and eating fish, literally take food from our mouths, is almost self-evidently ludicrous; (2) it assigns us, the human species, a greater right to eat and to make a living than other species. Cairns is careful not to remind the reader (who may, like me, be an agnostic, a humanist) that everything in the universe is God's work and that therefore nothing in the created universe is to be casually devalued, trashed: that is simply the axiom underlying everything the poem presents. Indeed, it is why the speaker can be compassionate even with the hypothetical killer of the harbor seal. The killer is human. All of us humans can be, at times, one-eyed. Cairns can imagine how a one-eyed killer might feel. He can imagine the temptation to evade moral responsibility, accountability.

The poem goes on in this vein, saying over and over, in its almost friendly tone, "I know how you feel; I know how you might on a whim wound a harbor seal with a rifle and then go off and let it suffer a slow death." "A seal's eyes are liquid anyway, / and alert right to the end." Cairns is even considerate enough to a hypothetical killer to offer an additional bit of armor against compassion, against remorse. If the killer had stuck around to watch the seal die and had thought that maybe the seal was crying—not to worry. It probably wasn't crying: "A seal's eyes are liquid anyway." A seal's eyes always look as though they are crying. Cairns then immediately points out how the rationalization that seals always look as if they're crying deconstructs itself. The natural "crying" look is the look of a creature "alert right to the end," therefore the seal was probably suffering if it *wasn't* actually crying. It was "alert." The next sentence pursues the same deconstructionist tactic. The sea mist that would supposedly prevent the seal from suffering if the seal dried out would actually prolong the seal's suffering by prolonging its half-life on the beach. Then comes the sentence that is the poem's apex: "You don't have to believe / any of this." You are free to ignore any fact that might make you feel uncomfortable. You are free to ignore the feelings of any seal, any person, any creature. You are free to believe, or not to believe, anything you choose. In a final gesture, placing the one-eyed vision of the killer in a wider and profoundly invidious perspective, Cairns *chooses* to do exactly what the killer chose not to do: he chooses to stay with the seal, to claim responsibility for it. Whether Cairns actually experienced the events that he relates here is irrelevant to the poem's force. Unlike the killer, he *imagines* being there. Moral responsibility is an act of imagination—a voluntary act which, as in this poem, one can choose to perform, even if the choice is painful. As Kierkegaard had put it, it's a question of "either/or."

"Harbor Seals" is but one example of the ways by which poets can retrieve some of the important subject matter which, as the American poetic milieu has evolved under the shadow—the lingering phantom ghost—of modernism, had been gradually, in a sort of de facto way, ceded to prose writers. The means by which poets can effect this retrieval are as various as the poets themselves. Stanley Kunitz's great poem "The Well-Fleet Whale" is one way. C. K. Williams's "Tar" is another, as are Philip Levine's "Buying and Selling" and Richard Howard's dialogue between Walt Whitman and Oscar Wilde, "Wildflowers." William Stafford's "Thinking for Berky" is another, as is Carolyn Forché's "The Colonel" and Sharon Olds's "Rite of Passage." To retrieve this subject matter will always mean going out into the "objective" world, sitting "down close to the idiot thing" and then discovering a rhetoric sufficient to treat of it. The enlarged content, which is the fuel for poetry will, in the hands of our best poets, dictate this rhetoric.

3

The Poetry of Moral Statement

The kind of knowledge dramatized by Cairns's "Harbor Seals" I would call "moral wisdom." Cairns presents it as a story. Although there are many advantages to presenting it narratively—moral wisdom is, like most of our accumulated human knowledge, inherently narrative—there is one potential difficulty. People may remember the story and the overall gist of the lesson it embodies, but they may not remember its extractable, paraphrasable "content" in exact wording. The story of Jesus, for example, is sprinkled with memorable sayings, "Let him who is without sin among you cast a stone" (the modern secular equivalent to this is "People who live in glass houses shouldn't throw stones"), and these sayings comprise a kind of abbreviated key—a reminder—about a story. Thus instead of retelling the whole story of the eighth chapter of John, verses 1–11 in order to illustrate the morality of some real-life situation one can simply recite the saying: "People who live in glass houses. . . ."

The issue of memorability is crucial to instruction—not just to moral instruction but to every kind of instruction, whether the lesson to be taught is the meaning of traffic signs, the quadratic formula, or the Golden Rule. Frost, in "Mending Wall," in the sentence "Good fences make good neighbors," mocks such sayings, yet even that saying has more than a little plausibility. It is potentially useful. A good proverb can summarize succinctly, in a mnemonically catchy formula, vast amounts of knowledge, the kind of knowledge as is found, for example, in "Murphy's Law" ("If something can go wrong, it will") and in other curious metaphorical statements such as "a stitch in time saves nine" and "watched pots never boil." If presented narratively or in a discursive argument, this kind of knowledge can take hours, days, even years to explain and, what is still harder, to justify. Compare, for example, the expression "putting the cart before the horse" to Hume's essay on "Necessary Connexion." A great deal of philosophical rumination is encapsulated concretely in the idiom.

The best poetry embodies, elliptically, a similar kind of knowledge. Think, for example, of how much psychological and epistemological theory are contained in Auden's sentence from "In Praise of Limestone": "The blessed will not care what angle they are regarded from, / Having nothing to hide." This is why I have come to value the poetry that I know word-by-word by heart, more than poetry that I have to reread in order to reexperience some imagistic effect or other. Such effects, of course—especially in contemporary poetry—can be dazzling, like this flourish from Roger Weingarten's "Apples":

> I'd clear the sawdust,
> bring one apple to a polish on my canvas apron
> and carry on until I couldn't see
>
> the nailhead or the stem
> as I flipped them between vertical studs
> into milkweed. . . .
>
> The memory of a brass
> plumb bob that caught the morning light
> swaying from a rafter
>
> little more this evening than a twinge
> in the shinbone I tapped
> with a hammer. . . .[2]

Every choice one makes during composition trades off one possibility for another. Usually, as Stanley Plumly pointed out in 1977, in "Chapter and Verse," where he distinguished between a poetry of "voice" and a poetry of "image," the possibilities are mutually exclusive. What has Weingarten had to trade off? As spectacular as "Apples" is to reread, it has two inevitable limitations. The first is epistemological. It praises some raw experience by presenting it with almost incredible vividness, describing it so well that the reader—this reader, at least—wonders why he isn't living that experience instead of merely reading about it. It's like reading about sexual love. Who wouldn't prefer to enact such love rather than read about it? Although words can enable one to remember an experience, to apprehend it more clearly; although they sometimes even enable one to glimpse something one had not known until trying to find the right words for it, words cannot, in the end, equal raw experience itself. This is what I think Robert Pinsky means in *The Situation of Poetry* when, speaking of the modernists, he says: "The premises of their work included a mistrust of abstraction and statement . . . and an ambition to grasp the fluid, absolutely particular life of the physical world, by using language. The premises are . . . *peculiar* [my italics] in themselves." [1]

The second limitation of "Apples" results from a trade-off built into free verse itself. Although its "fluid" structure can render realistically the movement of an individual's perception, free verse is usually not aurally as catchy as accentual-syllabic verse. It's not poetry that one can readily possess without carrying around the book. The poetry that we live with is likely to be more abstract, more epigrammatical, to contain explicit ideas.

Into this neutral air
Where blind skyscrapers use
Their full height to proclaim
The strength of Collective Man,
Each language pours its vain
Competitive excuse:

. . . .
All the conventions conspire
To make this fort assume
The furniture of home. . . .[3]

How many times have I, during international crises such as the
Cuban missile crisis, recited lines like these to myself as a kind
of consolation. They pinned down, with such deadly, calm accuracy, the drastic state of the world. It was language designed to
help one survive in an emergency. I could ruminate upon it as one
might ruminate upon a prayer. That is, in fact, what such language
may be: secular prayer. Auden's "September 1, 1939" consists, in
large part, of memorable plain statement, and, indeed, memorable
plain statement may be the most ambitious task in the rhetoric of
poetry. We all know by heart such statements: from the *Bible*—
"If a household is divided against itself, that household cannot
stand"—and from the works of Shakespeare—"The better part
of valor is discretion," or from Pope—"A little knowledge is a
dangerous thing." *Bartlett's Familiar Quotations* contains thou-
sands of such passages—in my edition forty-seven pages of them
from the *Bible*, and sixty-six pages of them from Shakespeare.

Such statements can be found in modern and contemporary
poetry as well: "Death is the mother of beauty," from Stevens's
"Sunday Morning"; or "human kind / Cannot bear very much
reality," from Eliot's "Burnt Norton." The Stevens sentence dif-
fers from the Eliot, because it contains obviously figurative language, and this distinction—between the literal and the figurative—raises a question of definition: What *is* a "plain statement?"
Or, put it differently: Which sorts of propositions qualify as "plain
statements" and which don't?

Instead of trying to apply rigorous criteria such as "The statement must not contain any imagery or metaphors, and it must
consist entirely of abstract words," I propose that we think of
"plain statements" as existing on a spectrum of propositions, a
continuum, one pole of which (I'll call it the "soft" pole) might be

epitomized by Stevens's "Death is the mother of beauty," the other pole of which (the "hard" pole) might be epitomized by Eliot's "human kind / Cannot bear very much reality." The criteria for measuring the "hardness" or the "softness" of a plain statement might be these. A plain statement in a poem is any statement which: (1) offers no physical description; (2) offers a tremendous generalization; (3) asserts significant meaning independent of the context in which it occurs (though it will, of course, pick up additional semantic resonance from that context). By these criteria, "Death is the mother of beauty" exists near the "soft" pole.

In the interval between "hard" and "soft," we might identify an intermediate range of statements, for example, from William Stafford's "Thinking for Berky," the sentence, "We live in an occupied country, misunderstood," where the word *country* can be regarded as either literal in meaning (America, the country where we live and where "Thinking for Berky" is set), or, figurative in meaning (any country where any citizen lives). Perhaps because I tend to believe that a middle ground is usually the strongest solution to competing claims, I prefer in poetry "plain statement" that is neither hard nor soft but somewhere in between, let's say "springy." To appreciate the full force of such "springy" plain statements, let us examine Stafford's statement in the context of the entire poem:

In the late night listening from bed
I have joined the ambulance or the patrol
screaming toward some drama, the kind of end
that Berky must have some day, if she isn't dead.

The wildest of all, her father and mother cruel,
farming out there beyond the old stone quarry
where highschool lovers parked their lurching cars,
Berky learned to love in that dark school.

Early her face was turned away from home
toward any hardworking place; but still her soul,

with terrible things to do, was alive, looking out
for the rescue that—surely, some day—would have to come.

Windiest nights, Berky, I have thought for you,
and no matter how lucky I've been I've touched wood.
There are things not solved in our town though tomorrow came:
there are things time passing can never make come true.

We live in an occupied country, misunderstood;
justice will take us millions of intricate moves.
Sirens will hunt down Berky, you survivors in your beds
listening through the night, so far and good.[4]

"Thinking for Berky" is not unlike the lyrics to a good folk
song. I can easily imagine it sung, in an almost talking blues style,
to a guitar accompaniment. Like the lyrics of many folk songs,
the poem is end-rhymed. But, unlike folk-song lyrics, the poem is
even more effective *without* a musical accompaniment. It is a narrative, conversation poem of voice. One need only read it aloud
a few times—read it *knowingly*—to feel it take hold of the reading voice and almost bodily force one into eloquent speech. To be
sure, the poem is powerful when read silently, on the page, but it
is still more powerful when read aloud, whether alone or before
a live audience.

A poem, though, is literature, not oral performance: for it to
register its maximum effect read aloud, the audience must know
the text in advance. Otherwise, a line such as "We live in an occupied country, misunderstood," though plausible on first hearing, is
liable to go right past the listener, who hasn't had an opportunity
to dwell on its contextual implications. In art, every decision—in
this case whether between oral performance or silent rereading—
trades something off for something else. The maximum effect of
"We live in an occupied country, misunderstood," is primarily literary, not oral; for the meanings of that proposition are those
shades of meaning that one teases out of a statement by dwelling
on it for a while and by trying it in various contexts. Only by

rereading and rehashing these contexts—retrieving them from a page of print—can one fully savor the line.

In the first stanza, Stafford relates an experience familiar to us all. Hearing, late at night, sirens, he wonders what the occasion is. Most of us, "listening through the night, so far" and hearing sirens, probably think something like, "They pulled somebody over for speeding or drunk driving," or "They're pursuing some criminal who's trying to get away." Hard on the heels of that kind of speculation might come a thought such as, "Hope they catch the bastard." Stafford plays off these expectations, but the twist he takes is surprising: instead of distancing himself from the "drama," he makes it personal; it is "the kind of end / Berky must have some day. . . ." In stanzas two and three, he sketches what he knew of her life: Raised by violent, abusive parents, outside the margins of comfy, middle-class culture, Berky had to get away from home "Early," probably by taking some kind of menial job, something in "*any* [my italics] hardworking place." "But," like all of us, even "the wildest of all," she had a "soul" that was "alive, looking out" for "rescue." In the fourth stanza, Stafford muses on the fate of individuals. His own fate has, so far, been "lucky," the very opposite of "the kind of end / that Berky must have some day." "There are things time passing can never make come true" echoes the note of tragedy and necessity foreshadowed in the word *must* in stanza one. Why fate works out so darkly for some people is a mystery, one of the "things not solved in our town though tomorrow came."

Stafford's musing upon fate brings him (and the reader) to the poem's major discovery—"We live in an occupied country, misunderstood"—to the realization that, regardless of how "lucky" or unlucky one's fate, everyone feels, much of the time, as though he or she lived in a "country" that was "occupied" by callous authorities who cannot understand our inner lives, who cannot acknowledge the "soul" in each of us that is "alive." Kids feel "misunderstood" by their parents and their teachers. Adults feel "misunderstood" by the Internal Revenue Service or by the highway patrolman who pulls them over for speeding. Employees feel "misunderstood" by their bosses, and *those* bosses feel "misunderstood" by *their* bosses, and so on. Although our initial response to the line is that "We" refers to two people—you and I—that Stafford is asserting a sort of secret complicity with the reader (a complicity that gains force when we remember that Stafford himself, when he was a conscientious objector during World War II, surely knew he was "misunderstood" by a "country"), "we" (the readers) have been cunningly set up for an ambush—the poem's last sentence—where "we" becomes the grimly mocking "you survivors in your beds / listening through the night, so far and good." Perhaps the sentence shouldn't be paraphrased, but I will attempt to do so.

The paraphrase would go something like this: When "you" hear the sirens and distance yourself from a hypothetical victim, you "misunderstand" that person; but "You" and "We" are the same person. Nobody can be excused from the charge of indulging in the casual exercise of moral superiority. No matter how "misunderstood" or victimized "We" might feel, we victimize others in the same way that we are victimized, every time we let ourselves fall prey to a complacent detachment from their plight. To write off people's souls like this is to make them our potential (or actual) victims. "We" has a range of reference that is infinite, and it is also reflexive; for Stafford surely knows that by accusing "you survivors in your beds" of moral indifference, moral laziness, he is enacting the very sin of which he accuses "you survivors in your beds." The last sentence is not unlike Christ's injunction, "He that is without sin among you, let him first cast a stone at her," but with one crucial difference. The speaker is being sarcastic. He is not Jesus. He cannot pretend to be without sin. He can only mock himself for his own pride, for the vanity of presuming to make moral judgments about people's souls, while insisting, like an existentialist, on the painful value of emotional honesty.

"We live in an occupied country, misunderstood," in the context

of "Thinking for Berky," presents, in memorable form, something
like wisdom—moral wisdom. It is didactic (though not shrilly
so), and it suggests several principles of poetry that bear consideration. The first, a familiar one, is that though verse is now a
literary genre, it alludes to its oral origins more frequently than
the other genres do. Rhyme and meter are preeminently oral conventions, invoking an imaginary situation in which a speaker or
a singer is addressing a live audience. When a poem is explicitly
didactic, this sense of a poem being a public address will be correspondingly heightened: the pronoun "we" will be more likely to
occur, as well as a second-person plural "you." These are inevitable pronouns in public discourse that deals with publicly shared
knowledge. In such verse, there will be a greater likelihood of
plain statement, because what I have called "plain statement"—
a statement that offers a "tremendous generalization"—is almost
self-evidently "public" in nature. A final principle would be this:
because moral instruction is made to be memorized, and because
rhyme and meter are mnemonic aids, in didactic verse there will
be a greater likelihood of rhyme and meter. This is why rhyme
and meter usually lend most verse a public, somewhat oratorical
character, whereas free verse is inherently more private in character. As Timothy Steele has pointed out in *Missing Measures*:
that the subjectivity of most modernist poetry and the invention
of free verse historically coincide is no accident.

It is possible, of course, to write an effective didactic poetry
of plain statement in free verse; but it is hard. One successful
example of such a poem is Stephen Dunn's "Middle Class Poem":

> In dreams, the news of the world
> comes back, gets mixed up
> with our parents and the moon.
> We can't help but thrash.
> Those with whom we sleep, never equally,
> roll away from us and sigh.

When we wake
the news of the world embraces us,
pulls back. Who let go first?—
a lover's question, the lover
who's most alone.
We purchase a little forgetfulness
at the mall. We block the entrance
to our hearts.

Come evening, the news of the world
is roaming the streets
while we bathe our children,
while we eat what's plentiful
and scarce. We know what we need
to keep out, what's always there—
painful to look at, bottomless.[5]

The biggest risk a poet runs when deploying plain statement is
sounding prosaic. In an end-rhymed, accentual-syllabic prosody,
plain statement is comparatively easy to execute without risk-
ing descent into "prose," because, in much the same way that
the music of opera can dignify the stupidest plot, rich traditional
prosody can lend public grandeur to even the simplest and most
conventional idea:

Fish, flesh, or fowl, commend all summer long
Whatever is begotten, born, and dies.
Caught in that sensual music all neglect
Monuments of unageing intellect.

Four lines have inflated into twenty-five words a thought that
could be expressed efficiently (though less decorously) in five
words: "Animals don't reflect on life." Yeats was an operatic
poet. End-rhyming, accentual-syllabic verse hypes up its subject
matter. Such verse borders, almost always, on bombast or public
oratory, but at least it's easily distinguishable as "poetry" rather
than "prose."

Dunn's poem is equally distinguishable as "poetry," but for different reasons—not by sound but by structure, by the slight, agreeable surprise it produces in the way each idea leads to the next and, even more important, by the way these ideas are related. The poem's argument, though not surrealist, is not logical. The "news of the world" is like a "lover" with whom we sleep and live, coexist daily but "pull back" from when we "wake." Too much immediate contact with the world's "news," as with another person, even a lover, is "painful to look at," so we distract ourselves from the pain, deflect the world's immediacy by our daily routines of trivial amusements—knowing, all the while, "what's always there," but discreetly, in our conscious "waking" lives, averting our gazes.

The vast majority of poems deploying plain statement, however, use end rhyme; and the reasons for this are, as I have said, familiar. As scholars like Walter Ong have reminded us, before the invention of movable type, knowledge of all kinds was handed from generation to generation orally. The words that made up the knowledge of one generation had to be memorized by the next, by ear (e.g., "A stitch in time saves nine"). Poetry that attempts to pass knowledge on and to dramatize that knowledge will thus naturally be attracted to the mnemonic boost of rhyme, even though it can also be read "silently." This is especially the case with nonspecialized and nontechnical knowledge. Virtually all of our popular wisdom, be it secular—Leo Durocher's "Nice guys finish last" or Yogi Berra's hopeful "It ain't over till it's over," on the one hand—or sacred—the Sunday sermons of the local minister or of Oral Roberts and Jimmy Swaggart on television, on the other, is *oral* wisdom. Unless we attend a local church, this wisdom comes to us via television. If American poetry were ever to try to play a more significant, public didactic role than it does, it would have to compete with the TV sermon. Indeed, to watch such TV evangelists as Oral Roberts, Billy Graham, or Jimmy Swaggart in action may be to watch America's popular "poets" in action. Like skilled poets, they use all the time-proven poetic techniques in order to present whatever lesson they are giving in a charming way: rhyme, alliteration, surging parallel structures, repetition, "voice," even body language. The form of a sermon, moreover, is as conventional as the form of a sonnet.

The traditional sermon follows a three-part pattern: an elucidation of a Biblical text, the doctrine depending on it, and the application of the text to the contemporary situation. In Jonathan Edwards's "Sinners in the Hands of An Angry God," for example, the Biblical text is "Deut. xxxii 35, Their foot shall slide in due time." The text is explained in terms of its Biblical context—"In this verse is threatened the vengeance of God on the wicked unbelieving Israelites, . . . " and the application, like Stafford's turn toward "you survivors in your beds," is addressed to "you," the congregation: "You probably are not sensible of this; you find that you are kept out of hell, but don't see the hand of God in it, but look at other things, as the good state of your bodily constitution, your love of your own life, and the means you use for your own preservation. . . ." Edwards, who was, in my opinion, the first great American poet, uses every poetic, rhetorical technique to hold his congregation spellbound by means of sound and sense. His sonic techniques consist of rhythm and alliteration: "if God should only withdraw his hand from the floodgate, it would immediately fly open, and the fiery flood of the fierceness and wrath of God would rush forth with inconceivable fury. . . ." His imagery is diabolical: "The God that holds you over the pit of Hell, much as one holds a spider or some loathsome insect, over the fire, abhors you. . . ."

Millions of people in America attend weekly sermons. These sermons resemble, in significant ways, poems; and the ministers who deliver these sermons resemble poets. A preacher must carry out two charges—the same two that Horace in his *Ars Poetica* charged poets with—he must instruct *and* "delight." As Edwards's sermon illustrates, a good sermon does both. It thrills, through rhythm and imagery, its audience. It does this so well that its audience will heed instruction—no matter how depress-

ing: "Consider this, you that are here present, that yet remain in
an unregenerate state. That God will execute the fierceness of his
anger, implies that he will inflict wrath without any pity."

Most people look for moral instruction *somewhere*—perhaps
in church, perhaps in psychoanalysis, perhaps in some forms of
literature. But rarely in poetry. Most of the poets I know are clever
people with a good working knowledge of the world. They have
sophisticated advice to give to their friends, to their local government, to business associates. Yet they feel, perhaps rightly, that
they cannot give this advice in their poetry. Why is this? There
are three main reasons, I think. The first one has to do with the
nature of genre itself. As the genres have evolved to this historical
moment, the sermon and the newspaper editorial are the genres
that can best handle in the public arena strong moral opinion.
Poetry no longer needs to take on such a task. The second one is
fashion. When Pound and Eliot and the modernists refuted Victorian poetry, one of their main targets was Victorian didacticism,
the moral smugness of a culture and its literature that hadn't yet
been interrogated by such events as World War I. "Imagism" was
pointedly amoral, and it was opposed to ideas ("No ideas but in
things"). The modernist refusal to tell—its insistence on merely
"showing"—persists even now. But there is a third reason, and
this one interests me most: the sheer artistic difficulty that a poet
faces when trying to make a moral statement. To write a poem as
good as "Thinking for Berky" seems to me to be a feat of stagger-
ing proportions—possible, as Stafford shows us, but difficult, and
the reasons for the difficulty are apparent. The poetic language
bequeathed to us by the modernists tends to be private and specialized—not adapted for making large generalizations. Imagism
and symbolist aesthetics have all but entirely replaced memorable
plain statement (the kind Pope perfected): poetic "effects" have
replaced instructional substance.

As the conventions and decorum of symbolist/imagist poetics
exhaust themselves, however, we begin to notice, here and there,
symptoms of a counterreaction to what Robert Pinsky shrewdly,

in *The Situation of Poetry*, called "the Romantic persistence." We begin to see signs of the readmission of ideas into our poetry, together with the possibility of didactic content. The clearest of these signs is the occurrence once again of memorable plain statements in verse using end rhyme to give its propositions sticking power. Such a poem, by a poet far younger than Stafford, is Baron Wormser's audacious "The Fall of the Human Empire":

When a dog is struck by a car,
A civilization collapses. A bystander
Explains this lack of allegory
As the dog whines about its accidental pain,
Wobbles and lurches. It is a gray afternoon
In the city. This shorthaired mongrel
Is not a bomb or a lie.
Two cars stop, and a student on the way home
From the public library thinks of how
Chekhov could see the world through the eyes
Of a dog. "No one believes me"—
That is the miserable thought which is
The sonata of these confusions. Clarity
Is equivalent to pain in this world.
Even a writhing dog, who is not Chekhov,
Could tell you that. There needs to be
An official for this compromising situation.
There needs to be an economy.
Dogs are like habits. This one sobs
And tries to drag itself somewhere else.
In operas people sing with all their hearts
About a missing loveletter or a shoe.
The world cannot be quiet any longer
About this dog. The peril is too great.
Silence is a dictator who lets you live
Today so you can be killed tomorrow.
Don't fool yourself.
This dog is unimportant as you.[6]

In its turn toward the reader at the end to voice directly to us some moral instruction, this poem resembles "Thinking for Berky." Perhaps it is in the very nature of such poems—poems that attempt to reduce the threshhold between "art" and "life," between the poem as a reading experience and experience in "real life"—that they adopt a sermonic stance and directly address the reader at some crucial juncture, as if to underline the threshhold which, as long as the reader felt that the poem was about only a hypothetical situation, had allowed him to admire the poem as mere art, however poignant. In fact, Wormser is grimly conscious of this possibility when he contrasts suffering in art (opera) with actual suffering (the dog's): "In operas people sing with all their hearts / About a missing loveletter or a shoe." No accident that "shoe" sets up the poem's final rhyme, a rhyme (and the punch line it cinches) deferred for five lines before it's sprung, with the word *you*.

In his decision to risk plain statement—"When a dog is struck by a car, / A civilization collapses" and "Clarity / Is equivalent to pain in this world"—Wormser evinces his impatience not only with imagist/symbolist poetics and the fabrication of "art emotions"; he questions the raison d'être of art of all kinds, if it merely diverts (however grandiosely, like opera) our attention from actual suffering, from actual injustice: "Silence is a dictator who lets you live / Today so you can be killed tomorrow." As we encounter the ugly little word *dog* one final time in the last line, we realize how relentlessly that word has sounded throughout the poem— seven times (eight, if you count *mongrel* in line six)—about once every four lines, like a sour knell; and we are taken back up to the poem's title, "The Fall of the Human Empire." Humans sing. Dogs whine. Humans have art and civilization. Dogs don't. They can only writhe. Humans, like art, "lie." Dogs don't, but "No one believes them." The poem operates like an enthymeme, with some suppressed terms, and their argument is clear. The very "distancing" of experience—the rendering of experience in hypothetical terms—that enables art (and perhaps the entire "Human Empire," civilization) to happen is the same "human" tendency that could lead it to "Fall": "a bomb or a lie." Bombs and lies are alike. They distance their users from suffering, and they are the inventions not of dogs but of the fallen "Human Empire."

Our poetry would be insufferable, ludicrous, if all of a sudden every poem began to preach some doctrine or other. But it's no accident, I think, that the poets with the widest following in America—poets such as Allen Ginsberg, Adrienne Rich, Carolyn Forché, Wendell Berry, and William Stafford—often write poems that are didactic, poems with explicit moral content. A great many people in America *want* moral instruction. They want poetry with a "message." The didactic is a line of development which, if pursued artfully, might further enlarge the estate of our poetry.

Contemporary Verse Storytelling

I have suggested in my consideration of the poetry of moral statement that most of our accumulated human knowledge is inherently narrative. Probably the most challenging of Joseph Epstein's charges against contemporary American poetry is his complaint that it " . . . gives away the power to tell stories, to report on how people live and have lived, to struggle for those larger truths about life, the discovery of which is the final justification for reading."

Epstein's charge is, as any regular reader of poetry will recognize, exaggerated. Within the massive, industrial-scale production of American poetry there are excellent narrative poems; but because of the sheer scale of the industry and the infinitesimal proportion of excellence in the poetry being written *at any time,* the task of singling out good narrative poems is formidable. It is far easier to find a good novel to read than an equally good narrative poem. But if our poetry is going to appeal to the sophisticated reader who, in search of stories that will shed meaning on his or her life will turn automatically either to scripture or to a novel, it might do well to try more storytelling. As Robert Stone wrote in "The Reason for Stories: Toward a Moral Fiction," "Story-telling is not a luxury to humanity; it's almost as necessary as bread. We cannot imagine ourselves without it, because each self is a story." Stone uses the *Bible* as an illustration:

We in the Western world are what the Moslems call "people of the book." The prototypical book in this culture has been the Bible, . . . our context and our perceptions continue to be conditioned by the Bible's narratives. . . . For centuries we have been reflecting on peculiar things—like why Esau was disinherited, and how Abraham could have been ready to sacrifice his son—and asking ourselves: What does this mean? What is at the heart of this strange story? What can I learn from it? How does it bear on my situation?" [1]

Stone takes it for granted that storytelling is an intrinsically communal activity: "Fiction is, or should be, an act against loneliness, an appeal to community. . . ."

In his essay "Poetry and the Audience," [2] poet/critic Michael Ryan touches on the issue of communality and narration, too. Ryan quotes Odysseus in Book IX of *The Odyssey:*

I think life is at its best when a whole people is in festivity and banqueteers in the hall sit next to each other listening to the bard, while the tables by them are laden with wine and meat, and the cupbearer draws wine from the mixing bowl and pours it into the cups.

Ryan then points out that this kind of communal narrative enterprise, in which "the poet still had an essential and therefore prestigious social role" was rendered anachronistic and adventitious by the invention of the printing press. He quotes the historian Daniel Boorstein:

Before the printed book, Memory ruled daily life and the occult learning, and fully deserved the name later applied to printing, the "art preservative of all the arts." The Memory of individuals and of communities carried knowledge through time and space.

Similarly, Wendell Berry, in his essay "The Specialization of Poetry," sees storytelling as perhaps the most central task that literature undertakes:

But even more suggestive of the specialization of contemporary poets is their estrangement from story-telling . . . this weakening of nar-

rative in poetry—whether by policy, indifference, or debility—may
be one of the keys to what is wrong with us, both as poets and as
people.[3]

Berry's phrasing, "What is wrong with us, both as poets and as
people," sounds a bit cranky; but the question remains: Why, if
storytelling has such communal power, don't poets try their hand
at storytelling in verse more often?

The answer is not especially complicated. As Timothy Steele
has pointed out in *Missing Measures*, most of the tasks that storytelling takes on are handled more effectively in prose genres, by
the short story and by the novel, than they are in verse—*most,* but
not all. Before examining this issue more closely—whether there
be *any* narrative tasks that verse could handle better than prose,
and if so, which ones and why—let us speculate a little. First, let
us agree that "story-telling" is an inherently "oral/communal" (I
prefer "communal" to McLuhan's "tribal") art, even when the
story is in print. Second, although poetry (according to orthodox
wisdom) is the oldest genre and "oral" in its origins, let us recognize that storytelling is a much more "oral" art than contemporary
verse is. True, at a modern poetry reading, the audience, if suffi-
ciently trained, will pay more attention to the audio aspects of the
verse being read than they will to the audio aspects of most prose
when it is being read aloud. But the attention by the audience to
the *sound* of poetry is a quaint, sophisticated concession to an
anachronistic idea. The initiated audience think they are *supposed*
to pay attention to "sounds": they have been trained to. In fact,
however, most of the best poetry being written in America today is
made to be read first, heard second. Why? Because most contemporary poetry is "lyric," and "lyric," as Northrop Frye reminded
us in *The Anatomy of Criticism*, is an "overheard" utterance, as
if the solitary reader were eavesdropping on the inner life of the
solitary poet. Although the term *lyric* suggests "song," lyric is virtually silent, especially since the invention of "imagism." Images
are silent. A contemporary imagistic lyric evokes in the reader's

imagination not a voice speaking to a public, but a montage-like flux of visual associations and memory that is, in Pinsky's words, "interior, submerged, free-playing, elusive. . . ."

Prose fiction, on the other hand, is likely to involve its audience in a communal ambience—even when the audience is a solitary reader not in the physical presence of the narrator—because it consists of storytelling. Consider, for example, the famous opening sentences of *Pride and Prejudice:*

> It is a truth universally acknowledged, that a single man in possession of a good fortune, must be in want of a wife. However little known the feelings or views of such a man may be on his first entering a neighborhood, this truth is so well fixed in the minds of the surrounding families, that he is considered as the rightful property of some one or other of their daughters.

The inflections of a storytelling voice are so palpable, in the preceding passage, that it is as if we were being addressed directly, immediately, by somebody who is present. Of course, this example is not entirely a fair one, because it is not contemporary. Austen's storytelling voice, with its confident generalizations, is addressed to an audience that shares so many values and expectations that it might almost be regarded as a "community." That was another time, another place; but even in more recent prose narration, when that narration is at its best, we observe how the charm and authority of the storytelling voice enlist us, the readers, as complicit members in a communal situation of listeners. In the following passage from *The Sun Also Rises*, note the confidently knowing way that Hemingway slings around loaded terms like *snooty* and *nice boy*, assuming that all his readers will be familiar with their connotations:

> Robert Cohn was once middleweight boxing champion at Princeton. Do not think that I am very much impressed by that as a boxing title, but it meant a lot to Cohn. He cared nothing for boxing, in fact he disliked it, but he learned it painfully and thoroughly to counteract

the feeling of inferiority and shyness he had felt on being treated as
a Jew at Princeton. There was a certain inner comfort in knowing
he could knock down anybody who was snooty to him, although,
being very shy and a thoroughly nice boy, he never fought except in
the gym.

Both the Austen and the Hemingway passages, because they
are addressed to an imagined audience that shares the speaker's
values as well as all the nuances of his language, evince that "radical of presentation," which Frye, in *The Anatomy of Criticism*,
labeled "epos":

> I used the word "epos" to describe works in which the radical of pre-
> sentation is oral address, . . . *Epos* thus takes in all literature, in verse
> or prose, which makes some attempt to preserve the convention of
> recitation and a listening audience. . . .
>
> The connection between a speaking poet and a listening audi-
> ence which may be actual in Homer or Chaucer, soon becomes
> increasingly theoretical, and as it does so *epos* passes insensibly into
> fiction. . . .
>
> I shall make an arbitrary choice of "fiction" to describe the genre
> of the printed page.[4]

Frye goes on to locate "epos" and "fiction" with respect to other
literary genres:

> *Epos* and fiction make up the central area of literature, and are
> flanked by the drama on one side and by the lyric on the other. . . . In
> *epos*, where the poet faces his audience, we have a *mimesis* of direct
> address. *Epos* and fiction first take the form of scripture and myth,
> then of traditional tales, then of narrative and didactic poetry, includ-
> ing the epic proper, and of oratorical prose, then of novels and other
> written forms. As we progress historically through the five modes,
> fiction increasingly overshadows *epos*, and as it does, the mimesis
> of direct address changes to a mimesis of assertive writing. This in
> turn, with the extremes of documentary and didactic prose, becomes
> actual assertion, and so passes out of literature.[5]

When Frye says "As we progress historically" that "novels and other *written* [my italics] forms" replace "traditional tales," he is alluding to the invention of movable type and printing; yet he is careful to refer to *epos* as "a *mimesis* [my italics] of direct address." In the Austen and Hemingway passages that I have quoted, the author is not present before the reader. What the reader experiences is merely the "mimesis" of direct address; but so convincing is this mimesis that we, as readers, experience some of the pleasure of being part of the audience in an actual storytelling session. The pleasure is like that of listening to well-presented narrative material over the radio. Although we may be alone, our literary experience has, in some important sense, a communal feel—the very kind of feel, I think, that Michael Ryan longs for with such piercing nostalgia, when "the poet still had an essential and therefore prestigious role." Epos, despite the medium of print, *is* a viable, perhaps even communal, radical of presentation, one that we experience regularly when reading a good story. Such narration is usually in prose, though, not in verse. If there's a questionable link in Ryan's gloomy prognostication about the marginal position of "poetry" in America today, it is that he ignores questions of "genre." Good novelists, like Robert Stone, command large and literate readerships. They exert cultural influence. *Poetry's* "golden age," on the other hand, when its chief task was that of storytelling, happened before the invention of prose.

Why have the genres evolved as they have, assigning the task of storytelling to prose writers and the task of "lyric" to writers of verse? Was it—is it—to use Berry's words, by "policy, indifference or debility?" on the part of poets? Mainly policy, I think. Modernist poetics, as conceived and executed by Pound and Eliot, disdained any literature that smacked of the communal or even of the "common" (unless that literature was at least two hundred years old). Pound's disdain might be epitomized in the "Mr. Nixon" section of *Mauberley*, a section that mocks, in the figure of Mr. Nixon, the popular novelist Arnold Bennett. To be sure, Bennett, as presented by Pound, might have been the Sidney Sheldon or the Harold Robbins of his day. Most of the advice that "Mr. Nixon" dispenses to aspiring young writers is commercial (" 'And give up verse, my boy, / There's nothing in it' "); but Pound's disdain for Bennett's commercialism is only a part of his grander disdain throughout *Mauberley* for anything that smacks of the popular.

One result of this evolution of the genres, however, is that today it takes some searching to locate good narrative poems by a contemporary writer. They exist, of course, but the types of these poems suggest some of the reasons why narration in verse is more difficult than prose narration. Let us look at an example, C. K. Williams's "The Gas Station":

THE GAS STATION

This is before I'd read Nietzsche. Before Kant or Kierkegaard, even
    before Whitman and Yeats.
I don't think there were three words in my head yet . . .
. . . .
It's dawn. A gas station. Route twenty-two. I remember exactly:
    route twenty-two curved,
there was a squat, striped concrete divider they'd put in after a
    plague of collisions.
The gas station? Texaco, Esso—I don't know. They were just words
    anyway then, just what their signs said.
I wouldn't have understood the first thing about monopoly or
    imperialist or oppression.
It's dawn. It's so late. Even then, when I was never tired, I'm just
    holding on.
Slumped on my friend's shoulder, I watch the relentless, wordless
    misery of the route twenty-two sky
that seems to be filming my face with a grainy oil I keep trying to rub
    off or in.
Why are we here? Because one of my friends, in the men's room over
    there, has blue balls.

He has to jerk off. I don't know what that means, "blue balls," or
    why he has to do that—
it must be important to have to stop here after this long night, but I
    don't ask.
I'm just trying, I think, to keep my head as empty as I can for as long
    as I can.

.   .   .   .

Here's what we've done. We were in Times Square, a pimp found us,
    corralled us, led us somewhere,
down a dark street, another dark street, up dark stairs, dark hall,
    dark apartment,
where his whore, his girl or his wife or his mother for all I know
    agreed, for two dollars each, to take care of us.
Take care of us. Some of the words that come through me now seem
    to stay, to hook in.
My friend in the bathroom is taking so long. The filthy sky must be
    starting to lighten.
It took me a long time, too, with the woman, I mean. Did I mention
    that she, the woman, the whore or mother,
was having her time and all she would deign do was to blow us? Did
    I say that? Deign? Blow?
What a joy, though, the idea was in those days. Blown! What a thing
    to tell the next day.
She only deigned, though, no more. She was like a machine. When I
    lift her back to me now,
there's nothing there but that dark, curly head, working, a machine,
    up and down, and now,
Freud, Marx, Fathers, tell me, what am I, doing this, telling this, on
    her, on myself,
hammering it down, cementing it, sealing it in, but a machine, too!
    Why am I doing this?
I still haven't read Augustine. I don't understand Chomsky that well.
    Should I?
My friend comes back at last. Maybe the right words were there
    all along.
Complicity. Wonder.

How pure we were then, before Rimbaud, before Blake. *Grace.*
Love. Take care of us. Please.[6]

This poem imitates "epos" as stringently as possible in a literary
(i.e., in a *reading*) situation. Like all good storytelling, the narrative tactics are built around digressions and asides, hesitations, as
if the speaker were thinking out loud, finding his way ahead in
the story before our very eyes. "This is before I'd read . . . I don't
think there were three words in my head yet . . . I don't know, they
were just words anyway then . . . I wouldn't have understood,"
and so on. The story itself is nothing special. It couldn't be said to
have "plot" in E. M. Forster's sense of that term. Except for the
speaker, who was changed by the events that he relates, there are
no "round" characters. As in Chekhov's stories, the compelling
element of this story is its storytelling voice—the voice's know-
ingness, its willingness to defer judgment as well as information,
its agonized honesty (or should I say its *attempt* at honesty, its
attempt at insight while, at every turn, questioning itself): "What
am I, doing this, telling this, . . . but a machine, too! *Why am I
doing this?*" And when Williams says, "When I lift her back to me
now," we sense, in that verb "lift," the sum of the effort behind
every one of the rhetorical markers preceding it. The poem's real
drama is in the assembling—or should I say in the disassembling
and reassembling—of its alleged "story": it's in the problematic
of trying to tell a story. Not surprisingly, such deployment of
"asides" is characteristic of all good narration, the framing of the
ostensible story in terms of the storyteller's rhetorical situation,
as for example in "The Rime of the Ancient Mariner":

It is an ancient Mariner
And he stoppeth one of three.
"By thy long grey beard and glittering eye,
Now wherefore stopp'st thou me?

The Bridegroom's doors are opened wide,
And I am next of kin;

The guests are met, the feast is set:
May'st hear the merry din."

He holds him with his skinny hand,
There was a ship, quoth he.
"Hold off! unhand me, grey-beard loon!"
Eftsoons his hand dropt he.

He holds him with his glittering eye—
The Wedding-Guest stood still,
And listens like a three years' child:
The Mariner hath his will.

The Wedding-Guest sat on a stone:
He cannot choose but hear;
And thus spake on that ancient man,
The bright-eyed Mariner.

. . . .

The aim of Coleridge's tactic here is self-evident. Since the poem
is going to be read, and since Coleridge will probably not be
present to read it aloud, he invents a stand-in storyteller, and by
means of what amounts to a "costume"—"long grey beard and
glittering eye," a clutching "skinny hand"—he invests this stand-
in with all the demonic mystery and urgency necessary to "hold"
a listener, a reader. Reading Coleridge's "Rime," we watch "epos"
happening, as it were, onstage. We experience it vicariously, until
we get caught up in the story and forget the stage altogether.

"The Gas Station," on the other hand, strives for something
more difficult than Coleridge's "Rime." It strives for the reader's
immediate rather than vicarious experience of epos. In order to
do so, however, Williams had to trade off most of the characteristics of verse. Indeed, reviewing *Tar* in *Field*, David Young, while
praising the work, characterized it as "prose." Young is close to
being correct, but only close. Is there *anything* in that "poem"
which a "poem" can do better than "prose"? Why did Williams
preserve, in his rambling lines, the vestige of verse? I think that the

answer is because he wished to fuse the overall poetic *structure* of his utterance (which is like that of lyric) with the discursive advantages of prose. Hence, "The Gas Station" is a sort of generic hybrid. Like a novel or a short story, it stakes almost everything on its rendering of detail and on its storytelling voice. Like lyric, it is shorter than most short stories, is in the first-person singular, and describes an initiation experience—indeed, like most lyric, its structure imitates the very structure of an initiation experience, by circling back to its (now transformed) beginning (a list of authors). "The Gas Station" is lyric in a second sense, too. It does not have the feel of fiction, because, although largely in the past tense, it is about what the speaker is feeling *now,* as he speaks (sings), and only secondarily about the past events he describes.

The autobiographical "nowness" of the speaker's presentation in "The Gas Station" suggests that the differences between "poetry" and "prose" may be rather more profound (though less obvious) than the differences between "verse" and "prose." To make a good narrative poem, it is not enough simply to reset prose fiction into verse, even when that verse is deftly handled. Consider, for example, the following passage from *Dead Reckoning,* a novel written in blank verse, by Brooks Haxton:

Amy remembered where the weed patch was.
She couldn't draw a map or give directions
But she told Eddy she knew she knew the way,
Which he found difficult to believe.
At least it was something else to do besides
Stare out the window or into the tube.
God knows he had followed boot lieutenants through
Quang Ngai without their knowing anything.

He looked down to the muddy water where
Small whirlpools formed and closed at either side
Of the blade with every stroke.

                                What could you do?
You *could* go back to where the rice was flat

In the propwash from the Chinook and drag
Malinowski out of a hot LZ,
Which made you a hero with a medal to prove it.
Then how did you feel? Not much different, did you?[7]

The writing here is excellent, a bit reminiscent of Raymond Chandler or Ross Macdonald. The loosely blank verse is unobtrusive. Indeed, the novel's format, verse, seems entirely extraneous. The reader's reaction begins in curiosity ("It's in verse!"), changes to indifference ("So what?") when it becomes apparent that the verse serves no purpose—that the best way to read the novel is pretend it's in prose—and occasionally swerves into impatience ("Could you back off a little, please?") when Haxton, who is a good poet, tries adventitiously to exploit the seemingly arbitrary fact of the verse in order to create an effect or two. When he does, the result is a sense of rhetorical huffing and puffing—melodrama—as well as confusion because the rules of the game have been changed (momentarily) in the very middle of the game.

The blue dark of the sandstone, flecked and swirled
With tiny single grains of quartz, looked
Cryptic as a night sky.

                    Dark, then.

                            Dark
And heavy beyond the property of stone,
Saturated with the dead weight of a man

.   .   .   .
This was the monolithic ax that Underwood
Turned slowly in his hands, inspecting it
For the communication vouchsafed by the dead
Whom he would join before long, from whom,
Meanwhile, he sought word. But this was stone
And mute. This was the monolithic ax.[8]

"The Gas Station," staking so much on its mimesis of a speaker's voice and his immediate presence, represents one extreme on a continuum of narrative verse possibilities. As I have already suggested, in all successful storytelling, the storyteller will, now and then, allude to his or her own presence and to the process of storytelling itself. Such self-referentiality is more than a convention. It is inherent in the ideal storytelling situation. The narrator, in order to summon the spell of illusion and sustain it over a difficult interval, must now and then show his hand, the "mirrors and wire" that hold up the contraption, in order to encourage the reader to go along with him; but as we investigate along the narrative continuum, away from epos, we notice that immediacy of voice is traded off for other possibilities. As the beginning of Coleridge's "Rime" might suggest, one of these possibilities—perhaps the major possibility—is rhythmical, and has to do with the "musical" possibilities inherent in the ballad, possibilities which, I need hardly add, are traditionally displayed in *verse*, not in prose.

The most fundamental convention of verse has always been that it must maintain a conspicuous verbal surface. When accentual-syllabic prosody was the prevailing form of this convention—its normal form—poets could automatically fulfill the requirement. They could write about almost anything, and assume that their text would be recognizable as "poetry." Meter, by foregrounding each discrete syllable within the context of the "foot," enabled a poet to draw attention to the verbal surface of his poem without resorting to conspicuous or forced figurative language. Reading Yeats, for example, we savor the sonic textures of his verses for their own sake; they usually have little if anything to do with a poem's referential "content."

Because the convention requiring of verse a conspicuous verbal surface is such a powerful one, it is inevitable that any general decline in the use of accentual-syllabic prosody will be accompanied by a corresponding increase in some other means of foregrounding verbal surface. And this is, in fact, what has happened in the free-verse lyric. There are two main ways of attracting a reader's attention to language in a poem: by means of sound, by means of sense. When the traditional, metrical, sonic means of foregrounding the verbal surface of verse is not available, a poet will turn, instinctively almost, to semantic means: stock lines with metaphors and similes, as if to compensate in the domain of "sense" what he has given up in the domain of sound. Whereas in the poems of Yeats we hardly ever encounter local tropes such as similes, in the contemporary American free-verse lyric the relatively high metaphoric density springs from the continuing anxiety by poets to fulfill the requirement to produce a conspicuous verbal surface—as if without it they would worry whether or not they were writing "poetry" at all.

This prosodic "law" of compensation, while fairly tidy when applied to the lyric, obtains more stringently when applied to narrative verse. As Timothy Steele has reminded us, the marriage of meter and narrative is as old as poetry itself. The heralded alliance of the so-called new formalists with something that bills itself as "The New Narrative" is either a publicity stunt or it is naive. The attachment of the prefix -new to contemporary narrative poetry is ludicrous.

Three conditions are placed on narrative verse. The first has to do with subject matter—the exigencies of exposition, characterization, and plot. (In the modern poetic milieu, none of these elements is regarded as inherently "poetical.") The second has to do with modern poetic structure, which, as we have already seen, in Williams's "The Gas Station," is predominantly the structure of the lyric: some material is presented, the poem develops this material, then makes its "turn," and the original material is re-presented in a sort of reprise, its meaning deepened, transformed by an accumulated context. In the genre of the short story, this technique is called "foreshadowing."

The third condition—the trade-offs between sound and sense necessary to maintain a conspicuous verbal surface—explains why most narrative verse, whether by Wordsworth, Browning, Robert Penn Warren, or Sydney Lea, rarely employs free verse. Because the subject matter of storytelling does not consist primarily of tropes, the prosody of even a contemporary narrative poem is likely to be traditional and formalistic—both to make the poem's language handsome and memorable, and to reassure both poet and reader that what he is reading is "poetry."

The ballad is one of the oldest narrative verse forms; and, the "new narrative-ists'" pronouncements notwithstanding, it is nowise a dead form. To observe a modern American "ballad" at its strongest, I invite the reader to consider Robert Penn Warren's great early poem "The Ballad of Billie Potts," a poem too long to quote here in its entirety, but a poem that combines the virtues of the best traditional ballads and country-and-western songs with the best of high-modernist poetry, in its eloquent free-verse digressions about the settling of the West, the nature of time, and the nature of the individual self. This ballad, parts of which have a catchiness not unlike Robert Service's "The Ballad of the Ice-worm Cocktail," has enough raw adventure to entertain a popular audience inured to TV dramas like "Gunsmoke"; but it also contains enough philosophy to engage an intellectual. The fact that this ballad, by a writer as famous as Robert Penn Warren, retelling a Biblical tale in a vernacular style, is not well known by the average, serious reader in America is virtual proof to me that poetry will never be genuinely "popular" in America; for if any single modern poem could be popular, it would be this one. The poem begins:

> Big Billie Potts was big and stout
> In the land between the rivers.
> His shoulders were wide and his gut stuck out
> Like a croker of nubbins and his holler and shout
> Made the bob-cat shiver and the black-jack leaves shake
> In the section between the rivers.
> He would slap you on your back and laugh.
>
> . . . .
>
> They had a big boy with fuzz on his chin
> So tall he ducked the door when he came in,
> A clabber-headed bastard with snot in his nose

And big red wrists hanging out of his clothes
And a whicker when he laughed where his father had a beller
In the section between the rivers.
They called him Little Billie.
He was their darling.

.   .   .   .

The plot of Warren's ballad is an ironic retelling of the story of the Prodigal Son as related in Luke, chapter 15. Billie's father and mother own and operate an inn. When a guest departs, if the guest had looked prosperous, they send a runner ahead, ambush the guest, and split up the spoils. One morning, when the runner fails to show up, Little Billie is enlisted as the substitute runner, but he muffs the killing, and his father sends him west to seek his fortune. When he returns, years later, a grown man, they don't recognize him. They kill him, go through his pockets, and bury him; but their neighbor, Joe Drew, who had recognized Billie, appears: "'And whar's Little Billie?'" After Joe Drew has left, Big Billie and his wife bring themselves to dig up the stranger's body. The unearthing of Little Billie is one of the most powerful passages of poetry, narrative or otherwise, that I know of:

She grabbled with her hands and he dug with the spade
Where the leaves let down the dark and shade
In the land between the rivers.
She grabbled like a dog in the hole they made,
But stopped of a sudden and then she said,
"I kin put my hand on his face."
They light up a pine-knot and lean at the place
Where the man in the black coat slumbers and lies
With trash in his beard and dirt on his face;
And the torch-flame shines in his wide-open eyes.
Down the old man leans with the flickering flame
And moves his lips, says: "Tell me his name."
"Ain't Billie, ain't Billie," the old woman cries,

"Oh, hit ain't my Billie, fer he was little
And helt to my skirt while I stirred the kittle
And called me Mammy and hugged me tight
And come in the house when it fell night."
But the old man leans down with the flickering flame
And croaks: "But tell me his name."
"Oh, he ain't got none, fer he just come riden
From some fer place whar he'd been biden,
And ain't got a name and never had none,
But Billie, my Billie, he had one,
And hit wuz Billie, hit wuz his name."
But the old man croaked: "Tell me his name."
"Oh, he ain't got none and hit's all the same,
But Billie had one, and he wuz little
And offen his chin I would wipe the spittle
And wiped the drool and kissed him thar
And counted his toes and kissed him whar
The little black mark was under his tit,
Shaped lak a clover under his left tit,
With the shape fer luck and I'd kiss hit—"
And the old man blinks in the pine-knot flare
And his mouth comes open like a fish for air,
Then he says right low, "I had nigh fergot."
"Oh, I kissed him on his little luck-spot
And I kissed and he'd laff as lak as not—"
The old man said: "Git his shirt open."
The old woman opened the shirt and there was the birthmark under
    the left tit.
It was shaped for luck.[9]

The ballad closes with a long Eliotian address to the reader about
fate and knowledge: "(. . . For the beginning was definition and
the end may be definition, / And our innocence needs, perhaps,
new definition, / And the wick needs the flame / But the flame
needs the wick. / . . . And you, wanderer, back, / . . . To kneel / With

the little black mark under your heart, / Which is your name, / Which is shaped for luck, / Which is your luck.)"

As Warren's "Ballad" might suggest—indeed, as the entire history of poetry would argue—when narration occurs in verse, it will most likely be within the most conventional forms. Perhaps even more conventional a narrative form than the ballad—particularly in a milieu like the present one, dominated as it is by the lyric—is the dramatic monologue. Such a poem is Sydney Lea's "The Feud," another poem too long (101 four-line stanzas) to quote in its entirety, but to my mind probably the best recent narrative poem by an American.

In an essay on "The Feud," Lea described, in 1983, the impulses behind his choice of writing a dramatic monologue rather than an autobiographical lyric:

> For some time I've wished that my poems would serve as coun-
> ters to narcissism, solipsism, self-absorption or -glorification or
> -laceration—my own as well as anything that Christopher Lasch
> would call "cultural." . . .
>
> It ["The Feud"] is, thank God-such-as-He-is, *not* autobiographical.
> The only thing that really happened is that a local family—known for
> slovenliness and violence—left a mess of deer guts on my lawn . . . ,
> my dogs gobbled them up, threw them up, and I got mad. . . .
>
> And yet it *is* autobiographical, contains a hidden personal alle-
> gory parallel to the overt and general one. And it is this fact which,
> however uncomfortable it makes me, impels the rest of my com-
> mentary. . . . my hostility to egotism/narcissism/solipsism/all of the
> above . . . may incline me to narrative *as a form*. . . .
>
> In 1980, my younger brother (second in line of five, I being the
> eldest) dropped dead of a stroke at age 35. And here is where that
> compelling (and still compellingly sad) thing fits into the poem's
> coded meaning. My brother was a black sheep, and I a white one.
> Thus I could judge his defects of character and behavior "quick
> as God."

> . . . We fought, as they say, like cats and dogs, . . . before we could
> begin to dismantle our moral artillery. And yet how much, almost in-
> evitably, we had in common. (I learned, for instance, enough to bring
> tears, that my brother was a closet poet.) His emotions and values
> were as vivid as my own, and how could I have considered it within
> my province to judge those values, and whether he had a right to
> them? Again like my narrator, I got the message a hard way: it took,
> literally, a stroke of domestic disaster to make me ask: What good
> have been your efforts to preach Truth, Goodness, Beauty? What do
> they mean *now?*[10]

In first-person singular storytelling, the imitation of epos, almost by definition, results in the equivalent to a dramatic monologue, and how "fictional" the speaking persona is will depend
entirely on how "fictional" are the events that the speaker relates.
Such "fictional" dramatic monologue is, in my opinion, one of the
most promising avenues that poets can take to attract readers who
are accustomed to seeking narrative values in prose fiction rather
than verse. Moreover, as "The Feud" illustrates, a poet need not
feature, as in the classic "dramatic monologue" such as Browning's "My Last Duchess," an interlocutor. When the speaker of
"The Feud" splutters his guilty explanations, the reader becomes,
vicariously, a sort of stand-in interlocutor:

> I don't know your stories. This one here
> is the meanest one *I've* got or ever hope to.
> Less than a year ago. Last of November,
> but hot by God! I saw the Walker gang,
>
> lugging a little buck. (A sandwich size.
> It *would* be. That bunch doesn't have the patience.
> I'd passed up two smaller, and in the end
> the family had no venison that fall.)
>
> I waved to them from the porch—they just looked up—
> and turned away. I try to keep good terms

with everyone, but with a crowd like that
I don't do any more than necessary.

.   .   .   .

I peeked out quick through the window as the Walkers'
truck ripped past, and said out loud, "Damn fools!"
The old man, "Sanitary Jim" they call him,
at the wheel, the rifles piled between

him and "Step-and-a-Half," the crippled son.
In back, all smiles and sucking down his beer,
"Short Jim" and the deer. Now Short Jim seems all right.
To see his eyes, in fact, you'd call him shy.

He doesn't talk quite plain. Each word sounds like
a noise you hear from under shallow water.
I didn't give it too much thought till later,
when the wife and kids came home, and wanted to know

what in Jesus' name that awful smell was,
over the road? Turns out that Walker crew
had left their deer guts cooking in the sun.
And wasn't that just like them? Swear to God. . . .

The rest of the poem, in this same, furious, breakneck, blank-verse, mutter, details the speaker's snowballing hatred of the lower-class "Walkers." Everything that goes wrong in his life he attributes to them, and he retaliates, secretly, with increasing viciousness. He tells how he "raked up all the lights into a bag / and after nightfall strewed them in their dooryard / with a note" and "signed my actual name." "There passed a week: they stove my mailbox up. / At least I don't know who the hell beside them / would have done it. . . ." The dispute might have ended there, except that one of the Walkers' dogs strayed onto the speaker's property. Next day he "drove it clear / to Axtonbury, to the county pound," claiming it was a stray, but keeping the identification. Nothing happens. Months pass. One day, the speaker comes out of "Ray Lawson's Auction" to find his tires slashed: "And still, / I judged it was the Walkers who had slashed / all four of my pickup's summer tires. / (Four months had passed.) And judged it quick as God." The poem's dramatization of how an individual can whip up in himself a deadly hatred and rationalize this hatred on the basis of no evidence at all—can bring hatred to a spit polish, "water it. . . . Night and morning," as Blake put it— is so authentic and moves with such momentum that it is terrifying and, for me at least, cathartic in the fullest sense of that term.

The speaker buys an apple and stuffs a rotten spot in it with rat pellets.

> Then went down that seventh night, as if it was
> another person who was going down
> inside the shed (because the person I
> believed I was kept up the sermon: "Nothing
>
> good from any feud," and so on),
> picked the apple down and put it in
> my pocket, and—the moon was full—began
> the uphill climb across the ridge. To Walkers'.
>
> Stopped for breath at height of land, I turned
> to see the house, where everyone was sleeping,
> wondered what they dreamed, and if their dreams
> were wild as mine become when moon's like that—

He feeds the apple to the Walkers' hog.

> . . . I don't know why, exactly,
> but I felt like watching as she took the apple
> *from my hand.* It wouldn't do to leave it.
> She just inhaled it, didn't even chew.

Then follows a passage that is the equal of the exhuming of Little Billie:

I don't know what you'll make of this:
I fairly marched back up across the ridge
as if I made that climb four times a day.
The air was cold and sweet and clear, the way

it is when you can see the moon so plain.
I walked on to a beat and sang the hymns
—or sang them to myself—I'd got by heart
so many years before: "Old Rugged Cross"

and "Onward Christian Soldiers" and "Amazing
Grace," and never noticed how the cold
had numbed my feet till I was back in bed.
No one woke up. I slept two righteous hours.

From his midnight adventure, the speaker comes down with pneu-
monia, which worsens until "In time, / there wasn't any use, I had
to go / down to the clinic, twenty miles away." When he returns,
his house is on fire, and his only son is trapped inside:

I stumbled to the shed and grabbed an ax

and put it to the ground to free the ladder,
but the ground just wouldn't give the damned thing up,
and every lick was like I swung the ax
from under water. I had no more force

than a kid or cripple. My kid, meanwhile, cried
from behind a big storm window, "Daddy? Daddy?"
It sounded like a question. I gave up
and tried to call up to him. I couldn't.

My words were nothing more than little squeaks,
and when they did come out, they were not plain.
And so my wife began to call the boy,
"Throw something through the window and jump out!"

He threw a model boat, a book, a drumstick.
He couldn't make a crack. I flung the ax.

It missed by half a mile. I threw again
and broke a hole, and scared the boy back in.

That was the last I saw him. Like a woman
sighing, that old house huffed once and fell.

The poem ends with the speaker having learned, as Lea would
say, "a hard way":

who's to blame? This time I'll let it go.
No man can find revenge for a thing like this.
They say revenge is something for the Lord.
And let Him have it. Him, such as he is.[11]

In *Missing Measures*, Timothy Steele writes:

It must be stressed that at just the time the novel was coming into
maturity, poetry was relinquishing territories it had long occupied.
The Romantic movement, though encouraging poets to explore new
areas of experience, also encouraged a spontaneous lyricism that
proved detrimental to the long poem. Evidence of this may be seen
in the unfinished extended works that are produced in the Romantic
period, works like *The Recluse*, *Christabel*, and *Don Juan*. These
efforts appear to have been propelled forward in brief bursts of intensity without the supports of the pedestrian but perhaps necessary
virtues of perspicuously arranged exposition. Indeed, in the Romantic and Victorian period, the short poem becomes the fundamental
poetic form. On occasion it is even urged that long poems are but
amalgamations of shorter works, as in Poe's remark, "What we term
a long poem is, in fact, merely a succession of brief ones—that is to
say, of brief poetical effects." . . . poets developed two responses to
the triumph of the novel. The first of these was to pursue a path . . .
in pure poetry. . . . The second response involved an effort to recover
materials increasingly claimed by prose fiction, and this response is
best exemplified by Browning, much of whose work aims at accom-
modating the narrative qualities and tones of the novel. For instance,
Browning's most famous long poem, *The Ring and the Book* of 1868–

69, attempts to do in pentameters what Wilkie Collins had been doing for a decade in his popular mystery stories.[12]

Of those attempts by the Victorian poets to compete with the novel, probably the most successful was George Meredith's *Modern Love*, a sonnet sequence of fifty pieces which, to my mind, is as grimly relevant to contemporary American life as any postmodernist American novel of the 1990s. A "modern" couple wakes up with the realization that their love has fled:

> By this he knew she wept with waking eyes:
> That, at his hand's light quiver by her head,
> The strange low sobs that shook their common bed,
> Were called into her with a sharp surprise.
>
> .   .   .   .

The sequence then, replete with many wry asides, documents how the couple attempts, almost mechanically, to infuse life into their marriage. In the final sonnet, Meredith states that it was their "modern" rational approach to "love" that doomed it:

> Thus piteously Love closed what he begat:
> The union of this ever-diverse pair!
> These were two rapid falcons in a snare,
> Condemned to do the flitting of the bat.
>
> .   .   .   .
>
> Their hearts held cravings for the buried day.
> Then each applied to each that fatal knife,
> Deep questioning, which probes to endless dole.
> Ah, what a dusty answer gets the soul
> When hot for certainties in this our life![13]
>
> .   .   .   .

In choosing to compose a narrative from a sequence of epiphanic moments, *Modern Love* anticipated the modernist triumph of lyric. Today, however, with modernism having used up the possibilities of formal experiment—the valorization of the "new"— the poetic sequence, instead of serving as a defensive accommodation to the novel, can serve as a lively alternative to an exhausted lyric tradition. An important example of such an alternative would be D. W. Fenza's *The Interlude*, a poem that, while incorporating significant elements from different genres, manages to refresh all of them. Like Meredith's *Modern Love*, *The Interlude*, in its ninety-two sections, tells the story of a modern marriage, in this case between a successful but self-centered, rather narcissistic corporate attorney and a lady who "sold high-tech / medical scanners. Her work often took her abroad, / to France; and she sent him postcards, but fewer / as months passed. . . ." The attorney dabbles in adultery and begins to drink too much. He is fired, goes on the skids, contemplates suicide, goes to AA, has to sell his home and rent a one-bedroom apartment and "After long unemployment" is "hired / by a small town newspaper." His father dies. "In the querulous rain, he walked to work, / treading his reflection again. Like a son, but / without father and mother, like his own man, / but still his wife's. . . ." After profound interrogation of his own life, he writes his wife, "Please return. I'm sorry. And I am yours." His wife "wrote and asked whether or not / he was ready to take her back and start a family." He writes her: "Dear X. I would like to have children." She returns, and they set out to have children:

> Open to the thrashing air, delirious rain and starlight—
> making love without birth control is like roaring off
> in a convertible with the roof down, rushing beneath
> a dubious sky, swerving along a three-lane highway where
> past, present, and future stretch for breathless miles, curving
> over vernal valleys and mountains. Thrilled and somber,
> they knew they were leaving themselves behind, that they
> were hurtling towards becoming a mysterious threesome.

> . . . .

What sets Fenza's poem apart from other verse novels such as Vickram Seth's *The Golden Gate* or Brooks Haxton's *Dead Reckoning* are two factors. The first of these is its generic allusiveness.

Like epic, it invokes, at its outset ("Section 0"), a muse: "An arch-
angel was marching before us—brandishing / a broken sword.
We followed him through dunes, . . ." This muse turns out to be
Archimedes. In its desert imagery and in its "quest theme," *The
Interlude* alludes heavily to *The Waste Land:*

> The hero of our tale, a lawyer whom we shall leave
> unnamed—he stared beyond his balcony windows.
> Over the city, the moon shone like a devalued coin.
> The month of April, for him, was a cruel burlesque,
>
> . . . .

The earnestness of the narration recalls Wordsworth's *The Pre-
lude,* and the urbane self-consciousness of some parts recalls Stevens's "The Comedian as the Letter C." Indeed, with its "happy"
ending, the poem is, though never funny, a comedy. What sets
Fenza's poem further apart from *Dead Reckoning* and *The Golden
Gate,* however, is that Fenza is able to produce with some regu-
larity, in medias res, passages that exhibit not only the luscious
verbal textures of the best verse, but the strangeness of poetry
itself:

> Sometimes pleasure lays itself down like obsequious
> pavements that keep the earth from rupturing into
> the anarchy of weeds, thorns, and burrs; and then
> your chest fills with the boring exhaustion of so many
> pigeons slumbering among charred rafters
> of an abandoned barn. The rain and ashes,
> as you recall a stranger unbuckling your belt.
> Regret is the after-shade of mere eroticism,
> the rain admonishing itself in the nearest puddle,
> a numbing penumbra the moon wallows within—
> a dark mirror, the cool lips of a shadow.[14]

The project of supplying a work of art with an extrinsic
apology for its being is, at best, dubious; for, as I am uncomfortably aware, the best, the most persuasive argument for any poem

must ultimately be the poem itself. This may be why, in most critical studies, scholars are attracted using short lyrics as examples. Indeed, the ascendancy of the lyric, and the coincidence of its rise with the rise of The New Criticism may be significantly related. The short lyric is ideally suited for "close reading." With a few exceptions, such as Eliot's *The Waste Land* (a poem tailor-made for New Critical explication, indeed, perhaps the "founding" poem of the movement), longer poems such as "The Ballad of Billie Potts" or *The Interlude* are generally not accorded the dazzling, lapidary critical treatment of lyrics like Wordsworth's "Lucy" or Frost's "Stopping by Woods": it is inconvenient. Longer poems, meditative or narrative, are thus placed, in the modern and postmodern critical milieu, at a drastic disadvantage.

What I hope the reader will understand is that my presentation of "epos," although it runs the risk of belaboring the obvious, of "reinventing the wheel," has not been intended so much to reveal a fresh possibility as to underline, implicitly and by contrast, the exhaustion and the narrowness of imagistic lyric decorum, at this literary-historical moment. The best narrative poetry not only gives us back the entire range of poetic conventions that had been curbed by the imagistic, show-don't-tell pieties of the modernist tradition. In its capacity to be discursive, digressive, and frankly *public*, it opens up to verse treatment kinds of subject matter that had conventionally been associated almost exclusively with prose genres.

Essay, Lyric, the Limits of Genre

In chapter 3 I attempted to suggest how our poetry might, by drawing on the mnemonic capabilities of verse, reclaim some of its neglected didactic potential. In chapter 4, I tried to suggest how poetry, by drawing both on "musical" and structural capabilities not as immediately available in prose as in verse, might reclaim some of the storytelling functions that seem to have become virtually the exclusive province of the novel and the short story. In this chapter, I would like to examine the question of whether our verse, by borrowing some of the structural conventions of expository prose, might reclaim some of the discursive subject matter currently regarded as belonging in the province of nonfiction prose.

In his *Rhetoric*, Aristotle, when giving instructions about how to appeal to various "types of character," describes the characteristics of the elderly in the following terms:

> The old . . . have been often deceived, have made many mistakes of
> their own; they see that more often than not the affairs of men turn
> out badly. And so they are positive about nothing; in all things they
> err by an extreme moderation. They "think"—they never "know";
> and in discussing any matter they always subjoin "perhaps"—"pos-
> sibly." Everything they say is put thus doubtfully—nothing with
> firmness. . . . They are slow to hope; partly from experience—since
> things generally go wrong, or at all events seldom turn out well. . . .

Aristotle might also have added that whereas lyric poetry is the natural genre of passionate outcry, expository prose is the genre of reflective expatiation. Certainly the older I become the more sympathetic I find myself with the nuance and multiple tonalities of expository prose, and the more strongly I suspect that this genre may be subtler than verse, an adult genre suited to a subject matter that one only begins, fully, to appreciate when initiated into the factual density and the contradictory nature of most adult experience. The *extreme* moderation that Aristotle makes fun of in the elderly, if mitigated only slightly, seems, if not like a virtue then like a necessity. It is moderation, in fact, which gives the best expository prose its charm—the capacity for urbane forms of qualification, for offering a balanced presentation of ideas. Indeed, it is the very rhetorical markers that indicate "balance"— terms such as "on the one hand" and "on the other hand"—which, Northrop Frye suggests in his *Anatomy of Criticism*, most characterize what he calls "non-literary prose." They seem endemic to it, endemic to a mode of writing that is specially adapted, Frye suggests, to particular kinds of subject matter. What is this subject matter? In Frye's words, it is "the outer world of *praxis* and *theoria,* social action and individual thought themselves." In other words, whereas the *outer* world—the world of political debate, of historical, social, and philosophical inquiry, as well as scientific investigation—is the subject matter that expository prose seems specially adapted to treat, the subject matter left over for poetry must encompass the "inner" world of "feelings." So ingrained are these assumptions that it was recently with some alarm and chagrin, that I found myself incorporating the blatantly prosaic expression "on the other hand" in a poem. The poem was called "Goodness." It noted that in kids' movies you can usually tell who the really evil characters are, because they are highly educated and use big words, whereas to sound "good" you have to speak in a bland, trite, rhetoric—"Golly, Mr. Wizard!"—and even to sound a little dumb. The reasons for this are, of course, complex—probably historical, and certainly Biblical. They include

America's edgy attitude toward its secular teachers, America's worship of machismo, America's ambivalent feelings about European culture, America's hatred of its own cities, America's nostalgic version of boyhood as a rural, Jeffersonian paradise of fishing, hunting, and cowboys and Indians, and America's idealization of its vanished frontier as a plunderable playground uncontaminated by books, uncompromised by what Huck Finn so cutely—Boys will be boys!—misspelled as S-I-V-I-L-ization. But my poem does not treat explicitly any of these themes. It can't, because they can be handled more efficiently and thoroughly in nonfiction prose than in verse. Nevertheless, the expression "on the other hand" demanded entry. It was necessitated by the subject matter. The tainted passage reads as follows:

It's no wonder that in every kid's t.v. show
where good and bad have been divided in two,
the bad guys get the slick vocabulary.
Darth Vader is smooth as a psychologist.
And the curdled school-marm in *The Wizard of Oz*,
that hag who hates dogs, pedalling
grimly, pedantically ahead through the sky,
hates with an exactitude
possible only in proper grammar.

My kids, though they may be truant at heart,
already are well-schooled enough that they
can instantly pick out evil on t.v.
God, they've been told, is like a winning coach.
He doesn't use too many fancy words.
He may sound tough. But he's always fair in the end.
In *Robin Hood*, on the other hand,
when the Sheriff issues his decrees,
they can tell he's up to no good.
His words are way too big,
his elocution too deliberate.

They know already, when a grown man licks
the taste of his own language like that
he can't be trusted. He's in politics.[1]

. . . .

"On the other hand." It's the utterance of a circumspect intelligence in the act of expatiating, of weighing alternatives, of qualifying its judgments. The speaker is not grieving over or celebrating
one alternative that is already a fait accompli: he is not singing.
He is thinking aloud. Similarly, the sentence "My kids, though
they may be truant at heart, / already are well-schooled enough
that they / can instantly pick out evil on t.v.," contains two quali-
fications whose significance can be appreciated if we imagine the
sentence having read, "My well-schooled kids can instantly / pick
out evil on t.v." That sentence would suggest only that "my kids"
had been trained to identify which clichés denote evil. "Though
they may be truant at heart" suggests something more complex—
some hypocrisy in their approach to those clichés. It suggests that,
although they contain a little original sin themselves, they glibly
pick it out in others. They are eager, like trained guard dogs, to
pass judgment on strangers. It suggests also, though implicitly, a
darker idea—that most moral schooling is inherently hypocriti-
cal, because it encourages people to externalize evil, to find it
always somewhere else, to check the knee-jerk "right" answer to
its location.

A second way in which the passage is qualified is in the prepo-
sitional phrase "where good and bad have been divided in two."
If the passage read, "in every kids' t.v. show, the bad guys get
the slick vocabulary," it would sound ominous, angry, accusatory,
like a passionate complaint, as if there were some conspiracy that
the speaker had noticed. "Where good and bad have been divided
in two" reminds the reader that the moral universe of popular
fictions is different from the moral universe where we dwell. In
the movie *Star Wars*, good guys can be distinguished from bad
guys. In the real world, few people, if any, are all good or all bad.

This information contains no novelty. It consists only of what, in Alexander Pope's words, "oft' was thought"; so the speaker tries to make it into something like Pope's "True wit," into something "ne'er so well expressed." The language is souped up by means of analogies, "smooth as a psychologist . . . like a winning coach," and by diction, "curdled school marm." The passage is further enriched by means of rhyme. Modern and contemporary lyric decorum favors a mimesis of intuitive, associative, affective mental process over logic. But the transition from "fair in the end" to "on the other hand" is a logical one, so the speaker uses the rhyme, "hand" in order to help the reader glide over the splice without thinking too hard—to camouflage a prose transition, a prose grammar. "In the end . . . on the other hand" comprise a tentatively asserted couplet. It reminds us, perhaps uncomfortably, of Augustan poetry, and it prompts one to speculate a little. Maybe the poetry of Pope is best described as discursive prose "gilded" by the frame of the heroic couplet, "verse essay" as David Young puts it in "Language: The Poet as Master and Servant," being careful to distinguish such "verse" from true "poetry," which is "lyric." Maybe Pope's *Essay On Man* is "non-fiction prose," as Frye would define it, made catchy, made, indeed, immemorial.

"On the one hand . . . on the other hand." Not only are such rhetorical markers, with their ability to balance and to qualify assertions, ideally adapted for certain types of discursive subject matter, but, Frye points out, they constitute the terms of a language which, though it looks abstract and literal, is really concrete and metaphorical. As Frye puts it:

> The link between rhetoric and logic is "doodle" or associative diagram, the expression of the conceptual by the spatial. A great number of propositions are spatial metaphors, most of them derived from the orientation of the human body. Every use of "up," "down," "besides," "on the other hand," "under" implies a subconscious diagram in the argument, whatever it is. . . . Very often a "structure" or "system" of thought can be reduced to a diagrammatic pattern—. . . We

> cannot go far in any argument without realizing that there is some
> kind of graphic formula involved. All division and categorization . . .
> signalled by "let us now turn to" or "reverting to the point made
> earlier," the sense of what "fits" the argument, the feeling that one
> point is "central" . . . , has some kind of geometrical basis.[2]

Wittgenstein meant something like this when, in his *Tractatus*, he
wrote, "We make to ourselves pictures of facts."

The segment of "Goodness" that I have quoted, then, must be
"prose." Not only does it place its various propositions within a
broad perspective by qualifying them in relation to each other. It
is "prose" because, unlike most poetry since 1800, the image that
it evokes is an abstraction: two, nonintersecting Venn diagrams.
One contains Darth Vader, The Wicked Witch of the West, The
Sheriff of Nottingham, anybody who, in a position of authority,
uses fancy words in a deceptive way for personal gain and to cause
deliberate harm. The other set contains Robin Hood, Peter Pan,
The Lone Ranger, Nancy Drew, as well as all, good, earnest, cute,
well-meaning kids—people who get along without the panoply of
institutional authority, but who, according to sentiment, are instinctively good and eschew hypocrisy. Like the terms *Good* and
Bad themselves, the two circles are so abstract as to be Platonic.

To appreciate the full charm of "prose," and some of its advantages, let's turn to a passage much better than mine. Let's look at
the very best modern prose possible, for example the following
passage from Lewis Thomas's *The Lives of a Cell*:

> A solitary ant, afield, cannot be considered to have much of any-
> thing on his mind; indeed, with only a few neurons strung together
> by fibers, he can't be imagined to have a mind at all, much less a
> thought. He is more like a ganglion on legs. Four ants together, or
> ten, encircling a dead moth on a path, begin to look more like an
> idea. They fumble and shove, gradually moving the food toward the
> Hill, but as though by blind chance. It is only when you watch the
> dense mass of thousands of ants, crowded together, blackening the
> ground, that you begin to see the whole beast, and now you can ob-

serve it thinking, planning, calculating. It is an intelligence, a kind of
live computer, with crawling bits for its wits.[3]

Some idea of just how exquisite, how delicate, even without its
surrounding context, this prose is may be appreciated if we compare it to a verse adaptation of it by the poet Robert Wallace, in
his textbook *Writing Poems* (1987):

Afield, a single ant of any kind
Cannot be said to have much on his mind;

Indeed, it would be hard by rights to call
His neurons, few, loose-strung, a mind at all.

Or say he had a thought half-way complete.
He is more like a ganglion with feet.

Circling a moth that's dead. four ants—or ten—
Will seem more like a real idea then,

Fumbling and shoving, Hill-ward, bit by bit,
As if by blind chance slowly moving it.

But only when you watch, in crowded dance
Around their Hill, a thousand massing ants

As black and purposeful as scribbling ink,
Do you first see the whole beast, see it think,

Plan, calculate—a live computer's bits
Of dark intelligence, its crawling wits.[4]

Wallace's verse adaptation is, in my opinion, an altogether excellent poem. In some ways it's better than the Thomas passage.
The poem's final expression, "crawling wits" gives me a shiver not
unlike the shiver I get from the last line of Yeats's "The Magi":
"The uncontrollable mystery on the bestial floor." In fact, the
Wallace adaptation has one obvious advantage over the original:
the couplets lend it a mnemonic catchiness, though occasionally

we may observe Wallace performing contortions in order to force a rhyme. Thomas's "blackening the ground," so shockingly accurate, has been altered to yield the poem's single weakest line: "As black and purposeful as scribbling ink," with its convenient end rhyme for "think." But the metaphor of the ants' group activity as that of "writing" mixes badly with—indeed it denies—the cinching metaphor of the ant colony as being like a computer; for the image of a pen scribbling in ink, although it embodies the notion of an intelligence, does *not* contain the notion of intelligence as consisting of discrete, seemingly isolate, "bits" of information.

Wallace has, however, traded off, for the sake of rhyme and meter, some much more important effects. He has traded off tone. The delicately modulated bloom of Thomas's prose style—a style which, to borrow Robert Frost's expression, "gets lost in translation" just as surely as the style of any good poem—is, in the Wallace translation, almost entirely blighted. Somehow, perhaps the result of the pacing or perhaps the result of small shifts of diction and other minutiae, the sense of puzzled, open-minded, curious, wonderment and humility before the natural world that gives the Thomas passage its power—our sense of Thomas's own mind weighing and qualifying as it observes, so that the reader seems to experience the actual process of fresh observation—is lost. The very neatness of the verse translation, due to its isolation from a larger prose context, creates a cocksure tone. This overassertiveness, in Wallace's adaptation, is due also, I think, to minute but crucial shifts in diction and syntax, and in differences between Thomas's and Wallace's placement and choice of those rhetorical markers so fundamental to prose. There is a world of difference between "a single ant" who probably doesn't "have much on his mind" and "a solitary ant" who probably doesn't "have much of anything on his mind." Wallace portrays the ant as an organism without an inner life. Thomas seems to leave the question of an ant's inner life more open, by implicitly comparing ants to humans. An ant may be merely "single"; a human is likely to be "solitary." An ant may not "have much" on his mind;

a human may not "have much of anything on his mind." To say
that a human "Cannot be said to have much on his mind" is to
imply that the specimen is either retarded or else empty. To say
that a human probably does not have "much of anything on his
mind" is far less pejorative, because it suggests a broader context
of mental activity: it is when *afield,* when busy in some specialized routine chore, that a human "cannot be said to have much of
anything on his mind" except the chore at hand. Thomas's placement of "afield" is crucial to the connotation of the passage. It
gives "afield" just the right emphasis. I could go on, in pedantic
detail, singling out the losses Wallace suffers, particularly the loss
in tonal modulation of the substitution of "As if . . . but only
when," in place of Thomas's "but as though. It is only when."
In each instance, the case I would make for Thomas's prose over
Wallace's verse would be the same: that the rhetorical markers
and the diction of the prose have the effect of subtly qualifying
each proposition by placing it in a larger context than would be
implied by the verse version. The urbanity and sense of wisdom
that the best prose affords derives, in large part, from its un-
hurried and generous admission into discourse of other possible
contexts. This is the opposite of lyric poetry. When Coleridge, in
his *Biographia Literaria,* argues that in poetry "every passion has
its proper pulse," he is assuming that the subject matter of poetry
deals, in large part, with "passion." But "passion," it would seem
self-evident, is a state of mind in which the subject rules *out* all
possible actions except one, in which mental activity proceeds in
a drastically limited context. It becomes obsessive. The speaker
of an impassioned lyric does not pause to put things into perspective. In fact, a condition for the success of lyric, and of song,
is that it convince the audience, during the interval of the song's
duration, to forget any other perspectives. As Barbara Herrnstein
Smith put it memorably, in *Poetic Closure:* "A poem must carry
its own context on its back."

The most fundamental tactic that lyric employs to do this is
through its assertion of closure. We can see this in the Wallace

version of the Thomas passage. By dint of its isolation, the discrete outline of the Thomas passage is foregrounded emphatically.
It exhibits a shape, development—one ant to four ants to a mass
of ants, culminating in a slam-bang ending whose finality is reg-
istered and reinforced by the couplet. But these are only apparent
advantages. In order to exploit them, Wallace had to trade off
something.

On the same page of my edition of *The Lives of a Cell*, two
paragraphs above it, we find the following passage:

> Ants are so much like human beings as to be an embarrassment. They
> farm fungi, raise aphids as livestock, launch armies into wars, use
> chemical sprays to alarm and confuse enemies, capture slaves. The
> families of weaver ants engage in child labor, holding their larvae
> like shuttles to spin out the thread that sews the leaves together for
> their fungus gardens. They exchange information ceaselessly. They do
> everything but watch television.[5]

Two pages later, we find the following paragraph, which is at least
as good as the first specimen from Thomas:

> Termites are even more extraordinary in the way they seem to
> accumulate intelligence as they gather together. Two or three termites
> in a chamber will begin to pick up pellets and move them from place
> to place, but nothing comes of it; nothing is built. As more join in,
> they seem to reach a critical mass, a quorum, and the thinking begins.
> They place pellets atop pellets, then throw up columns and beauti-
> ful, curving, symmetrical arches, and the crystalline architecture of
> vaulted chambers is created. It is not known how they communi-
> cate with each other, how the chains of termites building the column
> know when to turn toward the crew on the adjacent column, or how,
> when the time comes, they manage the flawless joining of the arches.
> The stimuli that set them off at the outset, building collectively in-
> stead of shifting things about, may be pheromones released when
> they reach committee size. They react as if alarmed. They become
> agitated, excited, and then they begin working, like artists.[6]

Thomas then goes on to give other equally startling examples of societies as organisms, bees and fish. So fascinating are these examples that, if I consider the entire chapter, I think that the very self-sufficiency of the initial passage, if asserted as a poem, though it's handy in the short run, may be, in the long run, a great loss, because it excludes such possibilities. I am uncomfortably aware of all the times when, setting out to write a poem, I felt a little smug, actually a little relieved that I was working in a genre which, because of its conventional encouragement of closure and self-sufficient structure, gave me the excuse to limit the number of facts that I had to know. I could rely almost entirely upon facts immediately at hand—upon the weather, upon my mood, upon some incident I had experienced. Not surprisingly, this is the subject matter we find, time and again, in that most conventional of poetic modes, the dramatic lyric: a personal experience that will comfortably fit within the frame of, let's say, around thirty lines of blank verse.

Not everything we experience in our normal lives, however, is inherently dramatic enough to interest others. The subject matter of the dramatic lyric, therefore, is even further specialized than is the subject matter of Thomas's prose. It consists of those experiences that we think of as "initiations," "rites of passage." Death and love are the most obvious examples of this type; but there are many others—every important first (and, perhaps, last) time we experienced something significant and dangerous enough that we drew upon our full emotional and intellectual resources: we were permanently changed by it, we would remember it for the rest of our lives.

One of the curious aspects of this type of experience—"the rite of passage"—is that it usually exhibits, even before it has been re-envisioned in poetry, conspicuous structure, a structure that is carried over into a poem and accentuated by artistic selectivity. Indeed, a "literary structure" seems often to be built into human experience itself. I am aware, of course, that there is a nontrivial sense in which, to use the current jargon, the nature of "the signifier" determines the nature of "the signified," a sense in which language and, presumably, literature, has a lot to do with how we perceive reality. The question of epistemological or ontological priority, however, is of little interest to me. Like the question of how to distinguish the influence of heredity from that of environment in human behavior, it is, I believe, inherently insoluble, at least by means of language. What I wish to emphasize here is only that the dramatic lyric has, because of its subject matter, a characteristic structure, and that this structure is significantly different from the discursive structure of nonfiction prose. It is a structure employing the artful limitation of context so as to dramatize, in a poem's very form, the process of an individual's coming into knowledge.

Although it is true that, as I suggested earlier, it is often expedient for a writer to exploit personal material in order to "get a poem out of it," good personal poetry exists for reasons other than expediency. All ideas—sophisticated scientific and mathematical concepts as well as personal thoughts—radically lose value, outside the context of some human story. As a reading of James Watson's *The Double Helix,* for example, makes plain, the process by which scientific concepts are arrived at is very significant. Such concepts, when they are approached biographically and historically, have intrinsic drama. Lewis Thomas himself recognizes this when, in his essay "Natural Science," he writes:

> The most mysterious aspect of difficult science is the way it is done. Not the routine, not just the fitting together of things that no one had guessed at fitting, not the making of connections; these are merely the workaday details, the methods of operating. They are interesting, but not as fascinating as the central mystery, which is why we do it at all, and that we do it under such compulsion.
>
> I don't know of any other human occupation, even including what I have seen of art, in which the people engaged in it are so thoroughly caught up, so totally preoccupied, so driven beyond their strength and resources.

Scientists at work have the look of creatures following genetic instructions; they seem to be under the influence of a deeply placed human instinct. They are, despite their efforts at dignity, rather like young animals engaged in savage play. When they are near to an answer their hair stands on end, they sweat, they are awash in their own adrenaline. To grab the answer, and grab it first, is for them a more powerful drive than feeding or breeding or protecting themselves against the elements.[7]

Thomas's description is familiar to all of us involved in creative work. There are famous testimonial anecdotes of poets: Housman cutting himself shaving, Emily Dickinson being patted on the head by her angel, and, of course, Roethke's post-compositional episodes of reeling, ranting, manic exaltation. Good poets recognize the value of the story behind what they personally know—of depicting the process by which they came to know something—because they recognize that, if we ignore the issue of utility, any form of knowledge, biological, mathematical, astronomical, sociological, psychological, despite its presentation as static fact or theory in some textbook, is actually narrative, that the *value* of this knowledge is contingent upon some kind of narrative structure.

The narrative structure of the dramatic lyric presents, in capsule form, the process by which some significant piece of personal knowledge is brought home to an individual: a rite of passage. Robert Frost's "Stopping by Woods on a Snowy Evening" might be considered a paradigm of this mode, but Frost's "Acquainted with the Night," a better poem, serves as a more instructive model:

I have been one acquainted with the night.
I have walked out in rain—and back in rain.
I have outwalked the furthest city light.

I have looked down the saddest city lane.
I have passed by the watchman on his beat
And dropped my eyes, unwilling to explain.

I have stood still and stopped the sound of feet
When far away an interrupted cry
Came over houses from another street,

But not to call me back or say good-bye;
And further still at an unearthly height,
One luminary clock against the sky

Proclaimed the time was neither wrong nor right
I have been one acquainted with the night.[8]

"Acquainted with the Night" is not so obviously "dramatic" as "Stopping by Woods. . . ." Its setting does not exhibit unity of time and place, and the action it depicts is almost entirely mental. The outline of its structure, though, is so distinct that it could almost be graphed or abbreviated. I prefer algebra to geometry, so I'll abbreviate it as a formula. It consists of three terms and is one possible abbreviation for a structure which, in both logic and in grammar, we associate with transitivity. $O = f(S)$. There is a troubled situation (S) which, as the realistic short story does, contains foreshadowing (f) of the events (in mathematical terms, the "operation") that will yield its outcome (O). In other words, O will be a transformed version of S. To put it in colloquial language: The poem begins by depicting a dramatic situation. The speaker is troubled, lonely, guilty, beset by trite negative thoughts, by thoughts often "acquainted with the night." What will he do? A luminary clock, unearthly and godlike, catches his attention, and proclaims "the time was neither wrong nor right," that all such human terms as *wrong* and *right*, like the time of day, are arbitrarily imposed upon the world. This realization is even darker than his earlier night thoughts: not only may the *arbitrary* quality of "wrong" and "right" be the true condition of "night"; but all the glum imaginings that he had toyed with earlier are colored by it, perhaps caused by this absolute condition, which is lack of faith. The night that he had been complaining about has taken on a whole new slant. It has undergone a transformation.

In the poem, of course, it is simply a word that has, through its reintroduction in a deepened context, been transformed, made progressively more figurative. But the poem's structure is, I think, approximately congruent with much human experience. As in all those experiences that constitute rites of passage, in this poem we feel that the knowledge of the speaker, by the end, like the transformation of the connotations of the word *night,* is irreversible, final. What is more significant, though, we notice that every single detail that preceded the poem's grim final knell "I have been one acquainted with the night" has been transformed as well. Rites of passage cause a person to re-envision permanently all his or her previous experience, in the light of whatever central event precipitated the "passage."

"Acquainted with the Night," then, is a beautiful, compressed paradigm of the process of coming into knowledge. If we compare it to the Thomas passage, to prose, we notice that Frost's very subject matter requires him to withhold information, to limit context in order to preserve the dramatic surprise which, with the poem's last line, produces the sudden enlargement that gives this type of subject matter its value, its quality of revelation. But such a careful limitation of context is the contrary of the multiple ways contexts unfold and qualify each other in good nonfiction prose. Indeed, I am tempted to wonder whether the two modes, the two strategies might not be mutually exclusive. The poet William Stafford stated this issue very well in an interview with Peter Stitt. Stafford said:

> Mostly I like to read prose now. I think I prefer prose to poetry. I think there are more talented people writing prose than poetry in our country today. Besides, poetry is trapped trying to do little adventitious, piddling jobs, even today when it seems to be flourishing. It is interesting, but it isn't overwhelming the way Pascal is overwhelming, or the way some writer like Alfred North Whitehead, who turns his first-class mind to a sustained communication project, is overwhelming. I think there are more prose projects now that are calling forth more the talents and the serious and sustained attention of writers than the kind of crochet work many of us are doing in poetry.[9]

I hope that Stafford is wrong. But I worry that he isn't, and I'm not the only one. If there were one underlying program in Robert Pinsky's *The Situation of Poetry,* it would be that in order to revitalize the "crochet work" of poetry, we must retake some of the territory seized by those "prose projects" that Stafford admires. My own so-called poem, "Goodness," which I have, with great trepidation, trotted out here as a specimen, may be, among other things, an attempt to test the compatibility of two modes—whether the impassioned, opinionated deployment of dramatic lyric, with its limited contextuality, is compatible at all with the calmer rhetoric of qualification and perspective, of nonfiction prose, with its discursive contextuality. The poem begins as dramatic lyric, contains a middle interval of proselike digression, and ends as dramatic lyric, when it returns to the setting where it opened and re-envisions its earlier materials. Here is the poem— I offer it only as a very tentative, embarrassing experiment, in its entirety—knowing that it is not "poetry," that it is prose set as verse:

GOODNESS

Brothels are built with bricks of religion
—William Blake

Though in a hurry, I linger
on the old widow Dettmer's porch,
cradling the dozen eggs I bought from her
while nodding and smiling, meeting her eyes,
letting her go on about the nice new minister
of her First Lutheran Church.
Good! Good! I find myself agreeing out loud
with her while marvelling
at how totalitarian such goodness is—
staunch enough to make even somebody
like me, who could never be
a party member to such orthodoxy,
smile and nod obediently like this, agree

to sound much dumber—*Yes!*
Good!—much more harmless than I am.
It's no wonder that in every kids' t.v. show
where good and bad have been divided in two,
the bad guys get the slick vocabulary.
Darth Vader is smooth as a psychologist.
And the curdled school-marm in *The Wizard of Oz,*
that hag who hates dogs, pedalling
grimly, pedantically ahead through the sky,
hates with an exactitude
possible only in proper grammar.

My kids, though they may be truant at heart,
already are well-schooled enough that they
can instantly pick out evil on t.v.
God, they've been told, is like a winning coach.
He doesn't use too many fancy words.
He may sound tough. But he's always fair in the end.
In *Robin Hood,* on the other hand,
when The Sheriff issues his decrees,
they can tell he's up to no good.
His words are way too big,
his elocution too deliberate.
They already know, when a grown man licks
the taste of his own language like that
he can't be trusted. He's in politics.
So when The Sheriff, like a new schoolmaster
leading his stolid posse of bailiffs
heads out toward Sherwood Forest again
to tutor the innocent trees, to fight
the propaganda that the sky is blue
they can hardly wait to watch him
get pelted home from his classroom of leaves,
swallow his own rich words.

Swell! I agree with Mrs. Dettmer again,
still longing to escape but dutifully

completing my payment of small-talk.
Her grandson's fresh, extra-large, 4-H Club eggs
are by far the best in town.
I wanted to be good, when I was ten,
and tried. But it was dull.
I couldn't abide the way old Mrs. Greer
went on about Joseph and his coat of many colors.
One beautiful spring morning I quit Sunday school.
Have a nice day. I recite it by rote,
my gaze fixed on her humorless eyes,
on her pulse—a pigeon The Sheriff
would have pulled from her throat—
as I manage that villainous polite smile
we reserve for those who are good—
those bastards who always leave us lonelier,
who accept us without question for
everything we are not.[10]

Can the conventional tasks of dramatic lyric be realized at such
a leisurely pace? Can the structure of dramatic lyric be interrupted
as it is in this example? I don't know. I'm not sure how compatible
the "prose" part of the poem is with the "lyric" part. "Goodness"
is fun to perform to a live audience. It's not unlike a stand-up
comedy routine. But in such a setting, I always introduce it with
a series of anecdotes that amplify the contexts for its subject matter. The farther I tow it out of the strict docks of poetry into the
bay of prose and toward the sea, where poetic decorum can be
thrown to the winds, the wider the attention I seem to command,
and the easier it is to make people laugh. Even a prose explication
of the "statement" that this so-called poem is trying to dramatize may be more provocative than its dramatization: that people
who, by enforcing an officiously pious, goodie-good demeanor,
who pressure us to be unnaturally polite, are practicing a form
of censorship, a furious denial of reality. It is the very opposite
of compassion. It is a denial that resembles the kinds of denial

practiced by every totalitarian government. Even when it is not causing human misery in Crusades, or in death squads, monolithic piety deeply violates us. The rage it inspires in us is close to hatred, because it is born out of our instinct for self-preservation.

Why can we say these things so much more easily in prose than in verse? Is it only a matter of the current literary environment, of convention? Or are the different potentialities for discourse inherent in each genre? Are the sources of these potentialities primarily environmental or hereditary? Both, I think; for there is no way to prescribe the limits of genre. We can know them only by testing them continually, by means of empirical experiments. Once we do this, we discover that the boundaries between the genres are significantly less strict than we had imagined.

We have seen in Don DeLillo's *White Noise* how effortlessly prose fiction can incorporate passages of lyric. We have seen in Baron Wormser's "The Fall of the Human Empire" how lyric, albeit it gingerly, can incorporate elements of sermon. And we have seen in David Fenza's *The Interlude* how verse can present in novelistic detail the story of a marriage. We have seen in the comparison between Lewis Thomas's *Lives of a Cell* and Robert Wallace's adaptation of part of it an unfavorable trade-off between the charm of the dramatic lyric, on the one hand, and the informational and tonal capabilities of the best nonfiction prose, on the other. In each of these examples, it is evident that the genres, while they exploit their own conventional expectations, are never "pure": They partake of one another, allude to one another, refresh one another, play off one another.

Of all the genres, nonfiction prose is, I think, the genre most resistant to verse treatment. In the hands of a great poet, however, there is perhaps no literary problem that is totally resistant. Robert Lowell's "For the Union Dead," for example, although it features marginally a lyric speaker, does not keep its primary focus upon the speaker's sensibility. Instead, it is an essay on American history—a verse essay. It is discursive, built around digressions. It values facts over feelings. Let us examine a second "verse essay,"

one perhaps as fully achieved as "For the Union Dead." Like the
Lowell poem, Robert Hass's "Palo Alto: The Marshes," is an essay
on history, in this case, California history; and like the Lowell
poem, it is a meditation:

PALO ALTO: THE MARSHES

—*For Mariana Richardson (1830–91)*

1.
She dreamed along the beaches of this coast.
Here where the tide rides in to desolate
the sluggish margins of the bay,
sea grass sheens copper into distances.
Walking, I recite the hard
explosive names of birds:
egret, killdeer, bittern, tern.
Dull in the wind and early morning light,
the striped shadows of the cattails
twitch like nerves.

2.
Mud, roots, old cartridges, and blood.
High overhead, the long silence of the geese.

3.
"We take no prisoners," John Fremont said
and took California for President Polk.
That was the Bear Flag War.
She watched it from the Mission San Rafael,
named for the archangel (the terrible one)
who gently laid a fish across the eyes
of saintly, miserable Tobias
that he might see.
The eyes of fish. The land
shimmers fearfully.
No archangels here, no ghosts,

and terns rise like seafoam
from the breaking surf.

4.

Kit Carson's antique .45, blue,
new as grease. The roar
flings up echoes,
row on row of shrieking avocets.
The blood of Francisco de Haro,
Ramon de Haro, Jose de los Reyes Berryesse
runs darkly to the old ooze.

5.

The star thistles: erect, surprised,

6.

and blooming
violet caterpillar hairs. One
of the de Haros was her lover,
the books don't say which.
They were twins.

7.

In California in the early spring
there are pale yellow mornings
when the mist burns slowly into day.
The air stings
like autumn, clarifies
like pain.

8.

Well I have dreamed this coast myself.
Dreamed Mariana, since her father owned the land
where I grew up. I saw her picture once:
a wraith encased in a high-necked black silk
dress so taut about the bones there were hardly ripples
for the light to play in. I knew her eyes
had watched the hills seep blue with lupine after rain,

seen the young peppers, heavy and intent,
first rosy drupes and then the acrid fruit,
the ache of spring. Black as her hair
the unreflecting venom of those eyes
is an aftermath I know, like these brackish,
russet pools a strange life feeds in
or the old fury of land grants, maps,
and deeds of trust. A furious, dun-
colored mallard knows my kind
and skims across the edges of the marsh
where the dead bass surface
and their flaccid bellies bob.

9.
A chill tightens the skin
around my bones. The other California
and its bitter absent ghosts
dance to a stillness in the air:
the Klamath tribe was routed and they disappeared.
Even the dust seemed stunned,
tools on the ground, fishnets.
Fires crackled, smouldering.
No movement but the slow turning,
of the smoke, no sound but jays
shrill in the distance and flying further off.
The flicker of lizards, dragonflies.
And beyond the dry flag-woven lodges
a faint persistent slapping.
Carson found ten wagonloads
of fresh-caught salmon, silver
in the sun. The flat eyes stared.
Gills sucked the thin annulling air.
They flopped and shivered,
ten wagonloads. Kit Carson
burned the village to the ground.

They rode some twenty miles that day
and still they saw the black smoke
smear the sky above the pines.

10.
Here everything seems clear,
firmly etched against the pale
smoky sky: sedge, flag, owl's clover,
rotting wharves. A tanker lugs silver
bomb-shaped napalm tins toward
port at Redwood City. Again,
my eye performs
the lobotomy of description.
Again, almost with yearning,
I see the malice of her ancient eyes.
The mud flats hiss as the tide turns.
They say she died in Redwood City,
cursing "the goddamned Anglo-Yankee yoke."

11.
The otters are gone from the bay
and I have seen five horses
easy in the grassy marsh
beside three snowy egrets.
Bird cries and the unembittered sun,
wings and the white bodies of the birds,
it is morning. Citizens are rising
to murder in their moral dreams.[11]

This poem, especially in its ninth and tenth sections, is strikingly
reminiscent of "For the Union Dead," and its bitter conclusion,
"Citizens are rising / to murder in their moral dreams," resembles
Lowell's more complex, hissing, "a savage servility / slides by on
grease." In verse, the format of numbered vignettes—a format of
which Stevens may have been the pioneer in poems like "Thirteen
Ways of Looking at a Blackbird," and Eliot in *The Waste Land*—

permits, even encourages the discursiveness we find in essays. The gaps between sections where, in prose, one would find a transition, are the equivalent to such prose rhetorical markers as "on the one hand . . . on the other," "nevertheless," and so on. The most haunting (because terrifying) passage in the poem is in the tenth section: ". . . a tanker lugs silver / bomb-shaped napalm tins toward / port at Redwood City. Again, / my eye performs / the lobotomy of description." Hass is indicting his own poem as well as modernistic, imagist convention in general. By showing rather than telling, by opting for "description" rather than the rendering of value judgments, the poetic language that he has been bequeathed cannot do justice to his own horror and outrage at the destruction of nature and of the Klamath tribe, or to his clear vision, in the family named "Richardson," of evil. "Palo Alto" is one example of how, by pressing the conventional limits of genre to the breaking point, a good poet will inevitably produce, in addition to overwhelming dramatic lyrics like Stafford's "Bess," poetry with (to use Joseph Epstein's words) "the power . . . to report on how people live and have lived, to struggle for those larger truths about life the discovery of which is the final justification for reading."

Conclusion

In an essay about the poetry of Ted Kooser, the poet/ critic Dana Gioia wrote:

> . . . what does an instinctively popular poet do in contemporary America where serious poetry is no longer a popular art? The public whose values and sensibility he celebrates is unaware of his existence. Indeed even if they were aware of his poetry, they would feel no need to approach it. Cut off from his proper audience, this poet feels little sympathy with the specialized minority audiences which now sustain poetry either as a highly sophisticated verbal game or secular religion.[1]

In these few sentences, Gioia has accurately summarized in the most succinct terms the issue underlying this book. As Gioia's comments suggest, the issue is, implicitly, a question; and, as the very phrasing of the "question" seems almost to demand, the answer to it is a paradox, a paradox around which the very best contemporary American poems are necessarily shaped, a paradox similar to the one noted by William Carlos Williams, when, in "Asphodel, That Greeny Flower," he writes:

> It is difficult
> to get the news from poems
> yet men die miserably every day
> for lack
> of what is found there.

Although most people approach these poems in the setting of the classroom and of the university poetry-reading, such poems are readily accessible. Subtle as they are, they do not, like the great early-modernist poems of Pound and Eliot, require excessive pedagogical indoctrination in order to be appreciated by the reading public. What are these poems like? One paradigm might be the opening poem of Philip Levine's *A Walk with Tom Jefferson*:

BUYING AND SELLING

All the way across the Bay Bridge I sang
to the cool winds buffeting my Ford,
for I was on my way to a life of buying
untouched drive shafts, universal joints,
perfect bearings so steeped in Cosmoline
they could endure a century and still retain
their purity of functional design, they
could outlast everything until, like us,
their usefulness became legend and they
were transformed into sculpture. At Benicia
or the Oakland Naval Yard or Alameda
I left the brilliant Western sun behind
to enter the wilderness of warehouses
with one sullen enlisted man as guide.
There under the blinking artificial light
I was allowed to unwrap a single sample,
to hack or saw my way with delicacy
through layer after layer of cardboard,
metallic paper, cloth webbing, wax
as hard as wood until the dulled steel
was revealed beneath. I read, if I could,
the maker's name, letters, numbers—
all of which translated into functions
and values known only to the old moguls
of the great international junk companies

of Chicago, Philadelphia, Brooklyn,
whose young emissary I was. I, who at
twenty had wept publicly in the Dexter-
Davidson branch of the public library
over the death of Keats in the Colvin
biography and had prayed like him
to be among the immortals, now lived
at thirty by a code of figures so arcane
they passed from one side of the brain
to the other only in darkness. I, who
at twenty-six had abandoned several careers
in salesmanship—copper kitchenware,
Fuller brushes, American encyclopedias—
from door to unanswered door in the down-
and-out-neighborhoods of Detroit, turning
in my sample cases like a general handing
over his side arms and swagger stick, I
now relayed the new gospels across mountains
and the Great Plains States to my waiting masters.
The news came back: Bid! And we did
and did so in secret. The bids were
awarded, so trucks were dispatched,
Mohawks, Tam O'Shanters, Iroquois.
In new Wellingtons, I stood to one side
while the forklifts did their work,
entering only at the final moment to pay
both loaders and drivers their pittances
not to steal, to buy at last what could
not be bought. The day was closing down.
Even in California the afternoon skies
must turn from blue to a darker blue
and finally take the color of coal, and stars
—the same or similar ones—hidden so long
above the Chicago River or the I.R.T.
to Brooklyn, emerge stubbornly not in ones

but in pairs, for there is safety in numbers.
Silent, alone, I would stand in the truck's
gray wake feeling something had passed,
was over, complete. The great metal doors
on the loading dock crashed down, and in
the sudden aftermath I inhaled a sadness
stronger than my Lucky Strike, stronger
than the sadness of these hills and valleys
with their secret ponds and streams unknown
even to children, or the sadness of children
themselves, who having been abandoned believe
their parents will return before dark.[2]

When I handed out copies of this poem to my poetry-writing
class, it created a minor sensation, because it triggered so instan-
taneously their memories of working: as stock boys in grocery
stores, hauling boxes in warehouses—of doing menial jobs in-
doors for such long hours that when they quit for the day they
were actually surprised to see the sun, to breathe fresh air. Like
Levine, in "Buying And Selling," they remembered experiencing
a sudden sadness, a feeling of having been somehow left out of
life, cut off from the world. One of the students remarked how
essential to the poem's ultimate force are its last two words, "before dark." That was exactly how he had felt as a child waiting
for his parents: innocently, faithfully believing that it is when it
gets *dark* that one is expected to be home.

Much more could be said of this poem—about the motif of
faithlessness (a motif running through Levine's entire book), fig-
ured in the word *abandoned* in the penultimate line—and about
the poem's real theme: economics. Levine's poem makes Pound's
writings about economics seem almost naive: "Buying And Selling" is the poem Pound might have been able to write, had Pound
ever worked at a real job.

More could be said, too, about the poem's rhetorical stance,
how it draws upon the conventions of different genres—lyric, nar-

rative, essay—and mingles them. It is through such generic loose-
ness—an allusiveness with respect to genre—that the poem is able
to include, with dramatic force, its unconventional subject matter. It is in its subject matter, its "content," that American poetry,
accomplished as it already is, can further enlarge its capability.

Notes

Introduction

1 Joseph Epstein, "Who Killed Poetry?" *Commentary* 86 (August 1988): 15.
2 Epstein, 16.
3 Epstein, 16.
4 Epstein, 18–19.
5 Epstein, 19.
6 Epstein, 19.
7 Timothy Steele, *Missing Measures* (Fayetteville: University of Arkansas Press, 1990), 9.
8 Brendan Galvin, *Seals in the Inner Harbor* (Pittsburgh: Carnegie Mellon University Press, 1986), 72.
9 Don DeLillo, *White Noise* (New York: Viking Penguin, 1985), 10.
10 William Stafford, *Allegiances* (New York: Harper & Row, 1970), 4.
11 Marilyn Krysl, *Midwife and Other Poems on Caring* (New York: National League for Nursing, 1989), 19–20.
12 Greg Kuzma, "The Catastrophe of Creative Writing," *Poetry* 148, no. 6 (1986): 354.
13 Epstein, 20.
14 Charles Altieri, *Self and Sensibility in Contemporary American Poetry* (New York: Cambridge University Press, 1984), 205.
15 Dana Gioia, "Notes on the New Formalism," in *Expansive Poetry: Essays on the New Narrative and the New Formalism*, ed. Frederick Feirstein (Santa Cruz, Calif.: Story Line Press, 1989), 168.

Chapter 1. The State of the Art

1 Wendell Berry, "The Specialization of Poetry," in *Standing By Words* (San Francisco: North Point Press, 1983), 4, 9.
2 Berry, 16–17.
3 Berry, 21–22.
4 David Wojahn, "'Yes, But' . . . Some Notes on the New Formalism," *Crazyhorse* 32 (Spring 1987), 64.
5 Robert Pinsky, *The Situation of Poetry* (Princeton: Princeton University Press, 1976), 162–63.
6 Pinsky, 3.
7 Steele, *Missing Measures*, 9.
8 Suzanne Juhasz, *Naked and Fiery Forms: Modern American Poetry by Women* (New York: Harper & Row, 1976), 205.
9 Alicia Ostriker, "American Poetry Now Shaped by Women," *New York Times Book Review*, March 9, 1986, 1.
10 Ostriker, 28.
11 Sharon Olds, *The Dead and the Living* (New York: Knopf, 1984), 66.
12 Carolyn Kizer, *Yin* (Brockport, N.Y.: BOA Editions, 1984), 20.
13 Kizer, 13–15.
14 Dave Smith, *The Roundhouse Voices* (New York: Harper & Row, 1985), 91.
15 Robert McDowell and Mark Jarman, *Reaper* 1 (1981): 3.
16 Brad Leithauser, "Metrical Illiteracy," *New Criterion* 1, no. 5 (1983): 41.
17 Leithauser, 46.
18 Feirstein, vii–xiii.
19 X. J. Kennedy, "Novel in verse is worth the hullabaloo," a review of *The Golden Gate*, by Vikram Seth, in *Los Angeles Times*; rpt., *Kansas City Star*, April 13, 1986, 8D.
20 *Reaper* 1, 52–54.
21 *Reaper* 1, 56.
22 *Reaper* 1, 62.
23 David Walker, *The Transparent Lyric: Reading and Meaning in the Poetry of Stevens and Williams* (Princeton: Princeton University Press, 1984), 18.
24 Altieri, 140.
25 Altieri, 212–13.

26 Hank Lazer, "The Crisis in Poetry," *Missouri Review* 9, no. 1
    (1986), p. 201.
27 Lazer, 203.
28 Lazer, 215.
29 Marjorie Perloff, "The Word As Such: L=A=N=G=U=A=G=E
    Poetry in the Eighties," *American Poetry Review* 13, no. 3 (1984): 16.
30 Perloff, 16.
31 Perloff, 18.

Chapter 2. The End of Modernism

 1 Michael Ryan, "Difficulty and Contemporary Poetry," *AWP News-
    letter*, November/December 1987, 14.
 2 David Young, "October Couplets," in *45 Contemporary Poems:
    The Creative Process*, ed. Alberta Turner (New York: Longman,
    1985), 245.
 3 Steele, 209.
 4 David Young, "Language: The Poet as Master and Servant," in
    A Field Guide to Contemporary Poetry and Poetics, ed. Stuart
    Friebert and David Young (New York: Longman, 1980), 166.
 5 Annie Dillard, "The Purification of Poetry—Right Out of the Ball-
    park," *Parnassus* 1 (Fall/Winter 1983, Spring/Summer 1984): 289.
 6 Dillard, 290.
 7 George Watson, "The Phantom Ghost of Modernism," *American
    Scholar* 54 (1985): 253.
 8 Watson, 260.
 9 Young, *A Field Guide*, 133.
10 Altieri, *Self and Sensibility*, 10.
11 Scott Cairns, *The Theology of Doubt*, (Cleveland: Cleveland State
    University Press, 1985), p. 32.

Chapter 3. The Poetry of Moral Statement

 1 Pinsky, 3.
 2 Roger Weingarten, *Shadow Shadow* (Boston: David P. Godine,
    1986), 3.
 3 W. H. Auden, *Collected Poetry of W. H. Auden* (New York: Ran-
    dom House, 1945), 57.

4 William Stafford, *Traveling through the Dark* (New York: Harper & Row, 1962), 16.

5 Stephen Dunn, *Not Dancing* (Pittsburgh: Carnegie Mellon University Press, 1984), 71.

6 Baron Wormser, *Good Trembling* (Boston: Houghton Mifflin, 1985), 53.

Chapter 4. Contemporary Verse Storytelling

1 Robert Stone, "The Reason for Stories," *Harpers*, June 1988, 73–74.

2 Michael Ryan, "Poetry and the Audience," *American Poetry Review* 17, no. 2 (1988): 7–20.

3 Berry, *Standing By Words*, 17–18.

4 Northrop Frye, *The Anatomy of Criticism* (Princeton: Princeton University Press, 1957), 248.

5 Frye, 250.

6 C. K. Williams, *Poems: 1963–1983* (New York: Farrar, Straus & Giroux, 1988), 215–16.

7 Brooks Haxton, *Dead Reckoning* (Santa Cruz, Calif.: Story Line Press, 1989), 87.

8 Haxton, 145–48.

9 Louis Untermeyer, *Modern American Poetry* (New York: Harcourt, Brace, 1950), 627–37.

10 Sydney Lea, "On 'The Feud,'" *Kansas Quarterly* 15, no. 5 (1983): 97–102.

11 Sydney Lea, *The Floating Candles* (Urbana: University of Illinois Press, 1982), 30–45.

12 Steele, *Missing Measures*, 88–90.

13 Arthur J. Carr, *Victorian Poetry: Clough to Kipling* (New York: Holt, Rinehart & Winston, 1960), 30–35.

14 D. W. Fenza, *The Interlude: Fables of the Twice-Fallen Angels* (Baltimore: The Galileo Press, 1989), 17.

Chapter 5. Essay, Lyric, the Limits of Genre

1 Jonathan Holden, *Against Paradise* (University of Utah Press, 1990), 43–44. First published by *Michigan Quarterly Review* 26, no. 3 (1987): 508–9.

2 Frye, *The Anatomy*, 335–36.
3 Lewis Thomas, *The Lives of a Cell* (New York: Bantam Books, 1974), 12–13.
4 Robert Wallace, *Writing Poems* (Boston: Little, Brown, 1982), 394.
5 Thomas, 12.
6 Thomas, 13–14.
7 Thomas, 118.
8 Robert Frost, in *The Poetry of Robert Frost*, ed. Edward C. Lathem (New York: Holt, Rinehart & Winston, 1969), 255.
9 William Stafford, quoted by Peter Stitt in *The World's Hieroglyphic Beauty: Five American Poets* (Athens: University of Georgia Press, 1985), 97.
10 Holden, 508–9.
11 Robert Hass, *Field Guide* (New Haven: Yale University Press, 1973), 24–27.

Conclusion

1 Dana Gioia, in *On Common Ground: The Poetry of William Kloefkorn, Ted Kooser, Greg Kuzma and Don Welch*, ed. Mark Sanders and J. V. Brummels (Ord, Neb.: Sandhills Press, 1983), 89.
2 Philip Levine, *A Walk with Tom Jefferson* (New York: Knopf, 1988), 3–4.

Selected Bibliography

Altieri, Charles. *Self and Sensibility in Contemporary American Poetry*. New York: Cambridge University Press, 1984. A useful, accurate survey of the field, in the mid-1980s.

Berry, Wendell. "The Specialization of Poetry," *Hudson Review* 38 (Spring 1985): 11–27. A seminal document in the reaction against modernist aesthetics.

Breslin, James E. B. *From Modern to Contemporary*. University of Chicago Press, 1983. Filled with journalistic detail. Particularly strong on Ginsberg and the Beats.

Breslin, Paul. "How to Read the New Contemporary Poem," *American Scholar* 47 (1978): 357–76. The most convincing repudiation of deep-image aesthetics and epistemology that is likely to be written.

Breslin, Paul. *The Psycho-Political Muse: American Poetry Since the Fifties*. University of Chicago Press, 1987. A stitching together of Breslin's review-essays. The chapters on Ginsberg, Ashbery, Black Mountain movement, and deep-image poetry are particularly strong.

Clausen, Christopher. *The Place of Poetry: Two Centuries of an Art in Crisis*. Lexington: University of Kentucky Press, 1981. Advances a thesis similar to Steele's in *Missing Measures*. Is ignorant of most contemporary American poetry.

Forché, Carolyn. "El Salvador: An Aide Memoire." *American Poetry Review* 10, no. 4 (1981): 3–7.

Frank, Robert, and Henry Sayre, eds. *The Line in Postmodern Poetry*. Urbana: University of Illinois Press, 1988. Essays by such writers as Perloff, Gilbert, and Scully, each with a different slant.

Halpern, Daniel, ed. *The American Poetry Anthology*. New York: Avon, 1975.

Hartman, Charles O. *Free Verse*. Princeton: Princeton University Press, 1980. At the time of its publication, the best extant study of free verse. It has now been rendered obsolete by Timothy Steele's *Missing Measures*.

Hass, Robert. *Twentieth Century Pleasures: Prose on Poetry*. New York: The Ecco Press, 1984. Urbane, personal essays on poetry, both national and international. A particularly sensitive, comprehensive essay on Rilke; a good essay on James Wright.

Holden, Jonathan. *Style and Authenticity in Postmodern Poetry*. Columbia: University of Missouri Press, 1986. Eleven essays describing the conventions that govern contemporary free verse composition in America.

Ingersoll, Earl, Judith Kitchen and Stan Sanvel Rublin, eds. *The Post-Confessionals: Conversations with American Poets of the Eighties*. Cranford, N.J.: Associated University Presses, 1989. Nineteen interviews conducted at the Brockport Writers Forum.

Jarman, Mark, and Robert McDowell. "Navigating the Flood," *Reaper* 1 (1981): 52–62. The earliest and the most plausible "manifesto" for a movement that has come to be called "The New Narrative."

Juhasz, Suzanne. *Naked and Fiery Forms: Modern American Poetry by Women*. New York: Harper & Row, 1976. The first critical study in America to define a distinct "women's" tradition in American poetry.

Lazer, Hank. "The Crisis in Poetry," *Missouri Review* 9, no. 1 (1986), 201–32. The clearest presentation that I have found of the agenda of the High Theorists with respect to creative writing.

Mazzaro, Jerome. *Postmodern American Poetry*. Urbana: University of Illinois Press, 1980. A stitching together of various reviews and essays. Journalistic.

Molesworth, Charles. *The Fierce Embrace: A Study of Contemporary American Poetry*. Columbia: University of Missouri Press, 1979. A collection of essays and review-essays, without any particular focus.

Ostriker, Alicia. "American Poetry Now Shaped by Women." *New York Times Book Review*, March 9, 1986, 1.

Ostriker, Alicia. *Stealing the Language*. Boston: Beacon, 1986. A polemic, arguing that the most important poetry in America is being written by women. To support this thesis, the author ignores much fine, *non-ideological* poetry by women.

Perloff, Marjorie. *The Poetics of Indeterminacy: Rimbaud to Cage.* Princeton: Princeton University Press, 1981. A detailed presentation of alternatives to conventional notions of genre in modern poetry and modern art.

Perloff, Marjorie. "The Word As Such: L=A=N=G=U=A=G=E Poetry in the Eighties," *American Poetry Review* 13, no. 3 (1984): 15–22. The clearest and the most persuasive account of this movement that is likely to be written, by America's smartest chronicler of experimental literature.

Pinsky, Robert. *The Poet and the World.* New York: The Ecco Press, 1988. A collection of essays by America's most important poet/critic.

Pinsky, Robert. *The Situation of Poetry.* Princeton: Princeton University Press, 1976. A sensitively written, book-length essay by a former student of Ivor Winters that comprises the earliest significant reaction against modernist imagist poetics.

Plumly, Stanley. "Chapter and Verse," *American Poetry Review* 7 (January/February 1978): 21–32; (May/June, 1978): 21–32. A brilliant justification for free verse, on the grounds of its urbanity and manipulation of tone.

Rich, Adrienne. "When We Dead Awaken: Writing As Re-Vision." In *American Poets in 1976,* edited by William Heyen, 278–92. Indianapolis: Bobbs-Merrill, 1976.

Rosenthal, M. L. *The New Poets.* New York: Oxford University Press, 1967. The book in which, concentrating on the poetry of Robert Lowell and Sylvia Plath, the term *confessional poetry* was coined.

Smith, Dave. *Local Assays.* Urbana: University of Illinois Press, 1985. Idiosyncratic essays by one of America's best poets. The chapters on James Dickey, James Wright, Richard Hugo, and Louis Simpson are worth the price of the book.

Spiegelman, Willard. *The Didactic Muse.* Princeton: Princeton University Press, 1989. A descriptive study, paying particular attention to Rich.

Steele, Timothy. *Missing Measures.* Fayetteville: University of Arkansas Press, 1990. The study of free verse—by an adversary of free verse—that renders Hartman's study obsolete. The ultimate repudiation of modernist poetics, this book regards modernism as an anomaly, an experiment that failed.

Vendler, Helen. *The Music of What Happens*. Cambridge: Harvard University Press, 1988. A descriptive study, much of which consists of Vendler's reviews in the *New Yorker*.

Walker, David. *The Transparent Lyric: Reading and Meaning in the Poetry of Stevens and Williams*. Princeton: Princeton University Press, 1984. A reader-response approach to modern poetry, arguing that the reader rather than the author is the protagonist of certain poems.

Young, David, and Stuart Friebert, eds. *A* Field *Guide to Contemporary Poetry and Poetics*. New York: Longman, 1980. Interviews and essays published in *Field*. Three of the essays are by David Young and set forth his aesthetics.

Index